THE JEMISON CAFE

ALSO BY JOHN HAYMAN

Research in Education (1962)

Evaluation in the Schools: A Human Process for Renewal
(1975, WITH RODNEY NAPIER)

Planning for Microcomputers in Higher Education:
Strategies for the Next Generation (1988, WITH REYNOLDS FERRANTE)

Bitter Harvest: Richmond Flowers and the
Civil Rights Revolution (1996)[1]

Doing Unto the Least of These:
The Story of Birmingham's Jimmie Hale Mission (1998)

Empowerment of a Race: The Revitalization of Black Institutions
(1999, WITH JESSE LEWIS SR.)

(POSTHUMOUSLY, WITH CLARA RUTH HAYMAN)

A Judge in the Senate: Howell Heflin's Career of Politics and Principle
(2001)[2]

---

[1]National Runner-up for the 1997 Robert F. Kennedy Award; Winner of the Alabama Historical
Association's 1998 Clinton Jackson Coley Award

[2]Winner of the Alabama Historical Association's Clinton Jackson Coley Award

THE JEMISON CAFE

Reflections on an Alabama Boyhood

John Hayman

NewSouth Books

Montgomery

NewSouth Books
105 S. Court Street
Montgomery, AL 36104

Publisher's Cataloging-in-Publication data

Hayman, John, 1929–1999.
The Jemison Cafe : reflections on an Alabama boyhood / John Hayman.
p. cm.

ISBN 978-1-60306-445-3 (paperback)

1. Hayman, John, 1929–1999—Childhood and youth. 2. Jemison (Ala.)—Social life
and customs—20th century. 3. Jemison (Ala.)—Biography. I. Title.

2016961074

Design by Randall Williams

Printed in the United States of America

Editor's Note

A lot of us reflect on our childhood with nostalgic memories of happy times involving family and friends. When discussions fall into the wishful category of "going back to the good ol' days" or "needing to go back to the way things used to be," further questioning will reveal "those days" were during the childhood years. Most likely, they were days of fun, free of responsibility, with little knowledge of the cruelties of the outside world.

Certainly, John Hayman reflected on his childhood with nostalgia. He felt blessed to have been so loved and cared for, yet he never desired to return to those days. He was always looking forward to life's next adventure. Part of John's nostalgia was his conviction that the family and world struggles he encountered during his growing up years in Jemison, Alabama, were instrumental in molding him into the adult he became. He saw the goodness of people, felt unity in despair, and experienced the universality of what being a community really means.

John loved Jemison with all his heart, and Jemison loved and respected John and his family in return. John never forgot "his roots," and he always took pride in telling others where he grew up. He was delighted to regale anyone who would listen with his Jemison stories.

John and his sister Barbara always felt they grew up in a magical time and place; to my knowledge, they never failed to discuss Jemison whenever they were together. I was fortunate to have been the recipient of these stories.

Through the years, John was encouraged to record his "Jemison stories" for posterity. Not only did the stories share personal and family information, but they included many of the townspeople who impacted the Haymans' lives, and they provided a history of how a small Southern town coped with and responded to the realities of harsh world conditions.

John spent several years recording his stories and confirming them with Barbara and others who grew up and/or lived in Jemison during the time period he remembered from his formative years.

His draft manuscript was sent to several people to review.

Unfortunately, John died October 19, 1999, before the manuscript was revised and finished. There was a lot of work yet to be done, and for several years afterwards, I was not emotionally able to take on the task of getting this book ready for publication.

Finally, sixteen years after John's death, I knew the time had come to bring this project to fruition. John and I were aware his stories comprised a history that needed to be preserved and told. Seventeen years later, you hold in your hands the results of this effort. I hope you read it, enjoy it, share it, and learn its subtle lessons.

The Haymans' house and the cafe building still stand alongside U.S. Highway 31. In later years, the original cafe building was heavily damaged when a car failed to make the curve on the road, and the cafe had to be replaced. Edith, John's mother, would never permit another eating establishment to occupy "her cafe." Barbara inherited the house, though she does not reside there. An eye clinic is in the old cafe building, which has been remodeled.

Notwithstanding all of his life's adventures outside of Jemison and Alabama, John's heart never left his hometown, and there it will always remain. John is reunited with his parents in Jemison's Pine Hill Cemetery. Sometime in the future, Barbara will join them there.

— CLARA RUTH HAYMAN HOLT

The Hayman family. From left, Barbara, John Luther Hayman Sr., John Jr., and Edith.

Top: house and cafe buildings. Bottom: Jack Sales.

Top: Jemison's Main Street in 1957—little changed from the period described in the book. Bottom: the Jemison train depot.

Top: the gin and blacksmith shop. Bottom: J. L. Hays's barber shop.

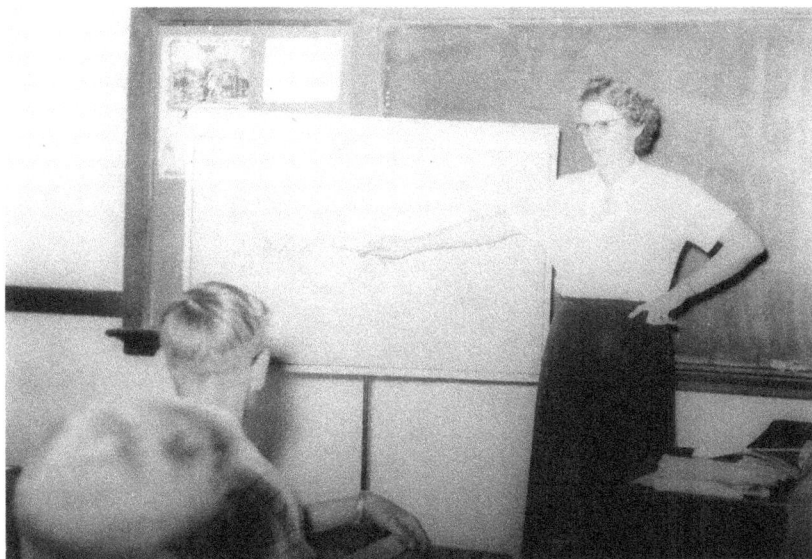

Top: teacher Edna Reynolds. Bottom: Edith Hayman in the Jemison Cafe kitchen.

Top: John L. Hayman Sr. conversing with Jesse James in the cafe. Left: Jerry James surveying the jukebox.

The author, John L. Hayman Jr., about 11 years old, by the Sinclair pump in front of the cafe.

1

Our '33 Chevrolet pulled into the parking space between the house and an old country-looking store building. It was May 1937, and the Haymans were arriving in Jemison, Alabama, to take up their new residence. It was my first time there, and all was strange and glorious. A truck filled with furniture followed the car into the parking space. A sign on top of the store building announced that this was "The Jemison Cafe."

I was seven years old, and my sister Barbara was eleven. We were moving from the Concord community, which is just outside of Hueytown in the Birmingham, Alabama, area. I was still wearing a cast, the result of being run over by a car two months earlier. The cast went from my stomach over both hips and down the right leg almost to the ankle. On the left leg, it stopped about halfway between the hip and knee, with holes in appropriate places.

Since I was immobile, my parents propped me up in a swing on the front porch. I watched the truck driver and his assistant unload our furniture and put it in the house. Meanwhile, my mother was very interested in the building next door; it housed a cafe and small grocery store, with a gas pump in front. It was to be the means of our economic survival. At least, that's what Mother and Dad hoped.

I didn't know it, but we were in a bad way—financially. The Great Depression was in its full fury, and times were hard. My dad had become physically disabled and had lost his job. Since Dad couldn't work, the burden fell on Mother. She had to succeed in the cafe. I mean, she really *had* to succeed since we were broke and had no other means of support.

I was innocent of financial concerns or any other worries, and I was curious about everything. I asked a lot of questions, but the men unloading the furniture weren't very interested in answering. Soon a black man came along; he was also curious about all the comings, goings, and these Haymans. He stopped abruptly when he saw this little white kid encased in a cast sitting in the swing. He asked my name, and I responded, "John." Before I had a chance to ask his name, he wanted to know what I had on my leg.

"It's a cast. A car ran over me back in March, and it broke my leg and my hip bone on both sides. It also cracked my head. It itches real bad under the cast, and I'll be glad when they take it off."

He laughed. He told me his name was Jack Sales and that he worked there—pointing to the cafe and meaning he worked for us—though we didn't know it at the time. He seemed to have quieted his curiosity, turned and told me he needed to get back to work. He said he needed to get out in the field and "do some things," and promised that when my cast came off I could help plow the mule and milk the cows. I liked his suggestion. He reinforced my notion that I was getting to be a big boy, and I figured I could plow and milk as good as anybody, though I'd never done either.

Jack Sales was one of the leaders of the black community in Jemison, and as I was to learn, he was a man who observed and thought deeply about a lot of things. Mom and Dad didn't know it when they bought the place, but Jack sort of came with the place. As it turned out, so did his family.

Our new place had eighteen acres, roughly in a square, and one side of it bordered U.S. Highway 31, a busy route which ran from Michigan to Mobile, Alabama. The house and cafe were on the highway. The entire acreage was inside the city limits of Jemison, a country town with a population of about 750.

UNFORTUNATELY, DAD HAD DEVELOPED severe health problems right in the middle of the Depression. He had worked since 1915 for a big lumber company in Brasfield, Arkansas. He thought he was fixed for life, but when the moment of truth came, his employer showed no mercy.

Being out of work and dependent on his wife was tough on Dad. He was from Texas and had been a tough "he-man" in his earlier years. He sometimes wore a .44 revolver on his hip, and he wasn't above getting in a fist-fight.

Dad was thirty-four when the U.S. entered World War I. As more and more of the workers left to join the service or work in a war industry, he had to take on more responsibility. In 1918, overwhelmed by it all, he had a nervous breakdown. His recovery coincided with the men's return, and things gradually returned to normal. Dad had given a lot to help keep the Brasfield mill operating.

As the 1920s came on, Dad's health and good spirits returned. He was a single, handsome man with a good job. He bought himself a fancy Chrysler car and was considered quite a catch by the ladies. Someone introduced him to a pretty young lady, Edith Summitt, and she caught Dad's eye. Romance bloomed.

MOTHER GREW UP ON a farm close to the rural community of Allendale, about ten miles southeast of Brinkley, Arkansas, and fifteen miles from Brasfield. Her father worked hard but just managed to keep food on the table. Mother did something unusual for a poor country girl in those days: she attended high school in Brinkley and graduated in 1922. Upon graduation she attended normal school for a year and earned a license to teach. Her first (and last) teaching job was in a small one-room school on the Cache River, a few miles from Allendale and just a short distance from Brasfield.

It wasn't long before Dad's courting paid off. They were married on Valentine's Day, 1925. She thought she had it made. She was married to a popular man with a fancy car and, in her eyes, a very fancy job. She was twenty years old, and he was forty.

SISTER BARBARA WAS BORN in 1926. I was born four years later, on December 3, 1929, a little more than a month after the stock market crash. For several years, things went well for the Haymans even though the Depression steadily worsened.

The mill where Dad worked was in the low country between the Cache and White Rivers, in the middle of a rich growth of virgin hardwood. The hardwood was cut, brought into the mill on small trains, and processed. The tracks for the train were regularly relocated, and the small steam engine was a source of great wonderment for youngsters in Brasfield. Finished lumber was shipped on the Rock Island railroad which ran through the middle of town.

By the mid-1930s, the mill had cut most of the useable hardwood trees. The company faced the same problems as everyone else in those hard times and decided to close the Brasfield operation. Different leaders in Brasfield were transferred to other plants, and Dad was to be in charge of a logging operation on the Warrior River, a few miles from Birmingham, Alabama. It was a sad day in 1936 when we left Brasfield. To us it was "paradise lost."

We moved. While Dad was trying to get a handle on his new job, he had a serious heart attack, and his arthritis grew worse. Soon it was obvious he could not continue his strenuous work as logging manager, and the company let him go. He had no retirement, no stock in the company, nothing to show for more than twenty years of faithful service and for sacrificing his health during the Great War.

In addition to being out of a job, Dad had lost all of his savings in the Depression. Before the market crash, he had $10,000 in a savings account. He also had about $12,000 worth of stock in Ford of France. In those days, it was a substantial amount. The savings bank failed as the Depression worsened, and Ford of France went bankrupt. Twenty-two thousand dollars quickly turned to nothing.

So THERE THEY WERE, like a lot of other people in that desperate time—no job, no money in the bank, and two children to feed. They tried selling violin lessons and were managing to survive, but both had to be away from home long hours each day. Barbara and I were left with an old lady who lived with us. It wasn't a happy arrangement, but it was working. During the Depression one did what one had to.

I upset it all and contributed to our general desperation by getting myself run over by a car. Barbara recalled the scenario.

"One Saturday we went to the neighbors. I was on skates, and John was behind me. We started home, and John was hit and run over by a car. I watched as the car dragged him forty feet. There he lay with blood everywhere and bones all bent in every direction. A man put him in his car and took him to the hospital in Bessemer. We didn't know where our parents were out selling the violin lessons. I think they were finally found by broadcasting on the radio. It was a terrible experience for me. I didn't like living in Concord anyway, and this really made me long for something different."

I was taken to Bessemer General Hospital, where I stayed eleven days.

I had a fractured skull and several broken bones, and had surgery to patch me up. A special nurse was there seven days and nights, and there were X-rays and other fees. The total bill was $102.

After I was released from the hospital, my parents decided they had to make a change in the way we lived. Dad had one remaining asset, an insurance policy with New York Life. My parents decided the ideal would be a small business with a house close by so they could look after Barbara and me. They also wanted a school in walking distance.

After exploring several possibilities, they purchased the house and cafe in Jemison. The day we moved was the first time Barbara and I had seen the place. Barbara was impressed, especially since we were moving from a house without a privy to a house with indoor plumbing. We hated the privy.

The previous owners promised to stay two weeks after we arrived and show Mother how to run the cafe and the store. Except for her year as a teacher, Mother had never worked for pay, and she knew nothing about the cafe business—or any other business. She needed some help in learning, at least, the bare essentials.

Too bad! The day we arrived, the previous owners left. The next day, Mother opened the cafe for the first time. She was on her own and had no idea what to do. Dad could give advice, but he was unable to contribute much physical labor. It was like being tossed in the deep end of the pool during your first swimming lesson; you either sink or swim. Only, with the cafe, there was no one to come to the rescue if we didn't make it. When Mother opened the cafe that first day, she *had* to succeed. Her heart flipped-flopped when the first customer walked in.

JEMISON IS IN NORTHERN Chilton County, the geographical center of Alabama, about forty-five miles south of Birmingham. In the mid-1800s, stagecoach drivers and other travelers stopped at that location to refresh themselves at some sweet-water springs. A railroad, later the Louisville and Nashville, was completed through the middle of the county in 1869.

About the time the railroad was completed, the town was named Jemison, after Confederate statesman Robert Jemison. It quickly became a farming center for the northern end of the county, and it had a successful lumber industry. Like other small towns in those days, it was self-sufficient, with a variety of stores.

Chilton County was formed after the Civil War and was also named after a Confederate general. The country was hilly and remote, and during the Civil War, a lot of Union sympathizers lived there. This led to hard feelings among different families. Next to Winston County, Chilton County had more Republicans than any other county in Alabama. Some were occasionally elected to local offices.

The county seat was Clanton, a larger town ten miles south of Jemison. Folks in Clanton thought of themselves as pretty high up socially, at least some of them did. This greatly irritated us bumpkins in the northern end of the county. We went to Clanton a lot because the courthouse and other county offices were there, and it had more stores than Jemison. Still, we resented the smug attitude of its residents. Clanton and Jemison were natural rivals in athletics, and we wanted nothing more than to beat them. Alas, Clanton had more resources and usually got the best of Jemison.

So, LIFE FOR THE Haymans started anew in Jemison. We had been through some bad experiences, but maybe things were looking up. Yet, Barbara was a worry-wart. She knew our folks had borrowed the money to buy the place. She didn't know until later that they had borrowed from their own insurance policy. All she knew was that they had borrowed the money and had to repay the loan. In those days, you didn't borrow anything if you could help it. She felt a lot of pressure not to eat up all of the profit, because we had to pay that money back.

But me, I didn't worry. I was wide-eyed and innocent. I thought life was wonderful. In Jemison, we had a nice house with an indoor privy. Also, we owned the Jemison Cafe, which was full of candy, ice cream, and hamburgers! What more could anyone want?

2

D ay two in Jemison began with Mother opening the cafe at 6 a.m. She was in a state of high anxiety. As it turned out, she had help. In marched Annie B., one of Jack Sales' daughters who had worked for the previous owners as a cook. I was snoozing away and happy as a lark. I'm not so sure about Barbara; she may have been sharing Mother's anxiety.

Mother didn't know the best time to open, but she figured she might serve some breakfasts if she opened early enough. A few customers came in, most out of curiosity. Annie B. helped as best she could. She knew some of the things to cook, but she had never been concerned with portions and costs and such.

One cow came with the place, and Jack came in about 7 a.m. to milk her. The barn was down a little hill behind the cafe. Jack brought the milk up in a bucket, and Mother strained it through a cloth. This gave us another commodity to merchandise, so milk became a specialty of the cafe at five cents a pint. The idea proved to be a great hit.

About eight, a striking young man came in and introduced himself as Bill Dubose. He also lived in Jemison, and promised to be one of our regular customers. Of course, Mother liked that. Bill confirmed that we had made the right decision to move to the fine town of Jemison.

In order to find out more about this "soon-to-be" regular customer, Mother inquired as to Bill's occupation. That could have been an embarrassment because Bill was unemployed like a lot of other young men, and he lived with his parents. But he didn't hesitate a second. He informed us he was an inventor and had several inventions on the drawing board that were sure to be a hit.

MOTHER ENCOURAGED BILL IN his work. He ordered a Coke, became our first Jemison friend, and, true to his word, he turned out to be a regular customer.

Bill was about thirty at the time. He was handsome with a pleasing personality. He was also very sharp mentally, and he had a lot of great ideas about things which ought to be invented. His problem was getting his ideas hatched in a practical way. He was also a great favorite with the single female teachers. He squired them around regularly and brought them to the cafe. We noticed he was always careful to make sure there were at least two females when he was squiring.

Some people came in for lunch that first day, and Mother managed to serve them. A few customers showed up in the afternoon, and several more came that night and ordered hamburgers. Mother didn't know how much meat to use. She made the hamburgers nice and thick to make sure the customer was happy. When she closed that night, there was actually more money in the cash register than the beginning of the day. Her anxiety subsided just a little.

MORE DAYS CAME AND went, and the cash register kept filling just a bit. That is, until the salesman came, and it was necessary to order more meat, buns, and other items. Mother realized that she had been making the hamburgers too thick, and she talked it over with Dad. She confessed her ignorance concerning portion control and lamented over how to make a profit. Dad assured her that all would be well. He told her that experience makes us all smarter. He suggested that she experiment, come up with a size that leaves the customer satisfied and would still make some money. He suggested she keep good records, and, never fear, he would be there to help. Mother was still skeptical that they could hold out. Again, Dad gave her the measure of assurance, "We'll hold out. The people you've met here like you, and you're giving them a fair deal for their money."

Barbara and I heard them talking about these things sometimes. It was over my head, but Barbara understood the critical nature of things, and, as usual, she worried. Dad told us that the key for the Hayman's survival was for the business to succeed. And, as long as we were here, we would have something to eat.

And we did. Mother, Dad, Barbara, and I ate all of our meals in the cafe. The kitchen in the house was used as a storage room.

Barbara remembers that things were tight. Mother kept saying that we shouldn't "eat up our profit." We could have one thing a day—a Coke, candy bar, or an ice cream cone. That was it, and the policy lasted several years.

As for me, I ate a hamburger or two every night for supper, and I thought this was great, especially if I could wash it down with a Dr. Pepper. Mother tried to get vegetables down me at lunch, but I managed to subvert her effort most of the time by filling myself with bread and butter while she was occupied with customers.

THE CAFE WAS IN a rectangular building about thirty feet wide and fifty-five feet long. The business part was in the front, with a storage room in back. An overhang extended about fifteen feet beyond the front door and provided a covered driveway next to the gasoline pump.

The kitchen area was separated from the front by a long counter which held pie cases, glass holders for cookies and such, and racks for peanuts and potato chips. The counter had three stools. Three booths extended the length of the room on one side, and the other side had shelves filled with canned goods. In front of the shelves were a handsome showcase and an ice cream box. With the table in the middle of the room, the seating capacity was nineteen.

THE FIRST BIG CRISIS came a few days after we arrived. The previous owners sold Gulf products, but Mother and Dad got a better deal from the Sinclair dealer and decided to switch. A load of Sinclair was dumped in the underground gas tank, but the sign identifying the brand had not been replaced. It was still big and round and orange and said, "Gulf."

A man stopped and had his car filled up. Gasoline was eighteen cents a gallon, and his bill came to $2. He pulled out a Gulf credit card to pay. Mother apologized, and explained that we had switched to Sinclair that week and the sign had not been changed. She could not accept Gulf credit cards. The customer was irate and, in a very forceful voice, told Mother she should have explained this predicament before he pumped the gas. He shouted that two dollars was a lot of money, and he didn't have that much cash—she would just have to give him credit.

This caused great consternation. Mother and Dad knew he was right, but they had decided to make it a strict policy that nothing would be sold on credit. Not only that, but the man's tag showed he was from Birmingham. They would never see him again if they let him get away. They still feared that bankruptcy might lurk just around the corner, and they didn't think they could afford the loss.

Dad explained to the man that neither he nor Mother intended this to happen, and he was not sure of the best thing to do. Dad suggested they get a hose and siphon the gasoline out of the man's tank, or to call the sheriff and let him handle it.

"What kind of stupid business is that?" the man responded. "I don't have time for you to siphon or to call the sheriff. You'll just have to accept my credit."

Dad was short tempered, and was about to answer in-kind when Mother stepped in, admitted their mistake, and stood her ground. She reiterated that the Jemison Cafe could not give him credit, and there was no choice but to call the sheriff. She also told the customer she had his tag number, and if he left, she would turn him in.

The man pulled out his wallet in a rage. "Here, here's two dollars. If this is the kind of dumb stuff you get out in the country, I'll never stop again."

He got in his car, slammed the door, and drove away in a huff. Mother had the two dollars, and she figured she would never see him again anyway.

Two days later a Sinclair sign was put up.

DIRECTLY ACROSS THE STREET from our new home was a marvel—a sawmill with accompanying lumber yard and sawdust pile. This looked like a great place to explore and to build roads and mountains, and I was anxious to get over there.

The sawmill workers rolled a log onto a carriage, and the carriage took the log directly into a large circular saw. By moving the carriage back and forth and gingerly adjusting the mechanism, the men sliced the log into several pieces. The person who worked the carriage had to measure correctly to get the boards the right width and cut no more wood than necessary.

I just couldn't wait to quiz them about how they did it. When I was able to go over there, I found they weren't at all eager to answer my questions. They were friendly but were adamant that I stay a safe distance from everything that moved. Their silence just made it more mysterious and enticing.

OUR HOUSE WAS ON the southeast corner of an intersection, and the cafe was a few feet over, with a parking space between the two buildings. U.S. Highway 31, the only paved road in town, ran in front of the cafe and house. A street, which went across the railroad tracks to town in one direction and to some houses in the other, intersected the highway. The street was dirt, like all the other streets in Jemison at that time.

The house had seven rooms and an enclosed back porch. Heat was provided by a fireplace in the living room and a kerosene heater in the bathroom. Because the four of us spent most of our time in the cafe during winter, someone would build a fire in the living room an hour or so before it was time for Barbara and me to go home, and the room would be comfortable when we got there. The bathroom was toasty warm.

Everywhere else was cold. Mother would warm up an old cast iron, wrap it in a piece of cloth, and put it under the covers at the foot of the bed. When we got in, we put our feet on the iron, and it warmed us from bottom to top. Being nice and cozy under those warm covers made for great sleeping, but there was a shock the next morning as we dashed for the bathroom.

DIAGONALLY ACROSS THE INTERSECTION from us was a filling station and garage. It sold Pan Am gasoline and was a great place for a boy to explore. The front room, where they collected the money, had tires and oil cans and such. In the large room in back, mechanics worked on cars, patched inner tubes, changed oil, and welded.

Next to the garage was a small wooden building which housed a cafe and the Greyhound bus station. It was run by Mrs. Leslie, the garage owner's wife, and it was always a source of concern and aggravation to Mother because it was competition. Mrs. Leslie made a little money from selling bus tickets and a little from her food. I liked her and even went in occasionally, though I had no doubt that our cafe was far superior!

Highway 31 curved sharply as it approached from the south, with the curve ending just before the highway reached our cafe. Unsuspecting drivers often came into the curve too fast. They lost control and created many interesting incidents at our end of town.

One day Mrs. Leslie was standing behind the counter in her cafe. A driver came flying up the highway and went out of control as he encountered the curve. Somehow he missed our building, swerved across the street, miraculously ran between the front of the Pan Am garage and its gas pumps, and went straight through the side of Mrs. Leslie's cafe. He came to a stop just in front of the counter. No one was hurt, but Mrs. Leslie was considerably startled. She wanted a customer but didn't anticipate one arriving quite this way.

A little to the south of us, in the middle of the curve, was a filling station. It was run by Tom Glass, and it had the only telephone in town. To make a call required going to Tom Glass's. If anyone wanted to call you, they called Mr. Glass's, and someone had to fetch you. Not very many folks talked on the telephone in Jemison.

Across the street from the house on our side of the highway was a large rectangular building which served variously as a grocery store, restaurant, garage, and what-have-you. I could see directly into the building's large back door from the bedroom window, and on days when I didn't have to get up, I lay in bed and watched what happened over there. Listening to the unsuspecting mechanics enriched my vocabulary considerably.

Up the highway was an assortment of houses, all with trees in the front yard and children about the ages of Barbara and me. The Leslie's house was just past the bus station on the west side. Next was an unusual stone house occupied by Seymour and Edna Reynolds. Seymour was a carpenter, and he had built the house with stones found in the vicinity. It had thick walls and was well insulated before anyone knew the value of insulation. Edna was a teacher with a fierce reputation among the students. The Reynolds had two children, Annette and Mary Edna, who were soon our friends.

A two-story wooden house occupied by Sam Reynolds and his family was next. Sam was Seymour's father, and most of his children were grown and out on their own. A son, Raymond, was in high school. One of the female teachers rented a room there. Sam and his wife slept downstairs, while Raymond and the young teacher stayed in bedrooms upstairs. Rumor had it that romance sometimes bloomed on the second floor.

Across from the Sam Reynolds' house were the Littlejohns. Mrs. Littlejohn was the postmistress, and her two sons, James and Charles, were in high school. Both of the boys were tall, athletic, and smart. Mr. Littlejohn was deceased.

On our side of the highway, were the Sims, the Densons, the Headleys, and the Petersons. From the very first, I had an eye for Alice Dorr Denson, but in the eight years between our arrival and the time they moved, I never had the nerve to tell her.

Altogether, more than a dozen children lived north of us on the highway, and that made it a great place to grow up. The parents were all solid, educated people. Two of them were teachers, and Mr. Peterson, who lived furthest north on our side of the street, was the school principal.

One of our favorite activities was to climb a chinaberry tree with a big limb growing out over the highway. Since Barbara was a "tomboy," she climbed, too. It didn't matter that she wore a dress all the time. We would get out on the limb, pick a handful of berries, and hide behind the leaves. When a "foreign" car came down the highway, we would throw chinaberries at it. The best kind of foreign car was one driven by Yankees, but one from another county would do. This was marvelous fun, but it came to an abrupt halt one day after an irate driver reported our game to the sheriff.

THE RAILROAD TRACKS RAN parallel to Highway 31 about two blocks west of us. On the other side of the tracks was a group of stores, houses, and other buildings. To us, everything on the other side of the tracks was "over in town." In the old days, just after Jemison was founded, the street through the middle of town was on the road connecting Birmingham and Montgomery.

Store buildings extended about two blocks on both sides of the street. One block had nothing but stores. At each end, buildings continued about a half-block in each direction. Altogether, there were about twenty stores, two barber shops, a service station, and a beauty shop. A small park with a well was next to the railroad tracks.

Across an alley behind the stores on the west side of the main street were the Masonic Hall and the Jemison Baptist Church, which Barbara and I attended. The ground floor of the Masonic Hall was used for a variety of purposes, such as meetings, pot-luck suppers, and an occasional movie. It was sometimes used by the health department to give shots, an activity which totally terrorized me.

Domino games and other activities fronted several stores on Main Street. Participants included unemployed males, youngsters, and during week days, boys playing hooky from school. The primary social center of Main Street was the post office, where Mrs. Littlejohn presided. She was a woman of great dignity. Everyone in town went in the post office several times a day, where they usually encountered a friend with which to talk. Mrs. Littlejohn and her helper were usually too busy to engage in casual conversation.

In 1938, the post office hosted a great event. James Farley, U.S. Postmaster General and Chairman of the Democratic National Committee, stopped by for a brief visit. Farley had been President Roosevelt's campaign manager and was a powerful national figure. I didn't know what all that meant. I just knew that banners were put up all over town, and everybody was really excited. Farley came in a big fancy convertible, escorted by policemen on motorcycles. It was very impressive. Aside from Farley, Mrs. Littlejohn was the center of attention, so Farley's visit was one of her finest moments.

ABOUT A MONTH AFTER we arrived, the doctor removed my cast. It was a moment of liberation. It freed me to explore the house, the cafe, the barn, the chicken house, the field, and when I could get across the street, the sawmill. I went down for the evening milking, but nobody asked me to participate.

I asked Jack a lot of questions about how he got the cow to come into the stall, the milking process, and such. He answered all questions patiently. When I asked if I could try my hand at milking, Jack told me I had to first get acquainted with the cow. He told me it would be nice if I talked and sang to her. Afterwards, when nobody was looking, I tried to be friends with her, but she wouldn't let me get close. We also had a mule and a bunch of chickens.

SHORTLY AFTER MY CAST was removed, I was sitting in one of the cafe's booths listening to the radio when a woman and a boy came in. The boy looked to be about my age, and this immediately got my attention.

The lady introduced herself as Ollie Dawson and her son, Junior. They lived across the highway in an apartment house. She smiled, and Junior returned my look of curiosity. Junior and I were soon fast friends. Junior's mother and dad, Marvin Dawson Sr., were divorced. Divorce was rare in those days.

Junior was an unusual boy. Even at that early age, he had discovered classical music, and he listened to it whenever he had the chance. Nobody in Jemison could figure that out. Even the elite mostly listened to swing and to the big bands.

Junior was creative, and I was always trailing him around watching the unusual things he did. One day he took me out in his back yard. He had built a dam on the small stream that ran behind the apartment house, under the highway to our side, and on through our pasture. The dam had some kind of contraption on the side like a water wheel used to grind corn and grains. Junior was pleased with himself.

The dam and water wheel were great, but there was a small problem. Jemison had no sewage system, and those of us fortunate enough to have indoor plumbing and lived next to the ditch piped our waste into it. Before the water wheel had been in operation many days, some choice items backed up behind the dam, and it was obvious to people in the vicinity that something was amiss. The mayor told Junior he had created a health hazard and the dam would have to go.

A FEW WEEKS AFTER we arrived in Jemison, a second great crisis occurred. Some men drove up in a truck and announced they were taking the showcase in the cafe. They claimed they had sold it to the previous owners several months before and had not been paid.

This was a valuable piece of furniture, and the threat threw Mother and

Dad into a panic. They told the men they couldn't have the showcase, but the men said they were going to take it anyway. Dad wasn't capable of a fist fight in his condition, but he was close to getting out the old .44 which he had stored in a drawer at the house.

Mother quietly sent someone to Tom Glass's to call the sheriff, and she managed to hold the men off until a deputy arrived. The deputy asked for proof of the men's claim. They didn't have it, and the deputy ordered them to move on. They made big threats as they drove away, but we never saw them again.

Mother would open at 6 a.m. seven days a week and stay open at night as long as there were any customers. The cafe had a juke box, from which we received a percent of earnings. Some of the boys would hang around until 11 o'clock at night playing their favorite songs. Mother never chased them away.

Pretty soon it was clear to Mother and Dad that we weren't going bankrupt. As Dad predicted, we were eating and paying the bills. The Jemison Cafe was taking care of us.

3

The back room in the cafe was used for storage. It included a table where some foods were processed and where the black customers were served. The water heater was also back there and was next to a cot where anyone could take a rest. One day Barbara and I were lying on the cot.

"Why is that roll of wire on the pipes?" Barbara asked. The hole in the wall where pipes went to the water heater was square and a good bit bigger than actually needed. I looked over between the tank and the wall, and sure enough, there was something gray in a coil lying on the pipes. I was about to pick it up when it moved!

"Yipes," Barbara yelled. "It's alive!" She jumped up and, moving close to the speed of light, called for adult help from the front.

It was a snake. Dad happened to be close by, and he managed to get it outside and properly dispatched. It was a harmless rat snake, but to Barbara and me, it represented pure terror. After that, we were more alert when we got on the cot.

RIGHT FROM THE START, Mother made sure we went to the Baptist Church every Sunday. Mother and Dad didn't go. Mother opened the cafe every Sunday because it was the busiest of the week. I don't remember Dad telling us why he didn't go to church, but one time I overheard him tell Bill Dubose that he figured he would get more out of reading a book.

The Baptist Church was an old wooden building constructed about the turn of the century. It was square, in a classic country arrangement, with the entrance on one side and a bell tower on the other. The church was one big room. When it was time to have Sunday School, a set of curtains, which hung on wires strung from side to side, were pulled, but we could still hear what went on in other classes.

The preacher at the Baptist Church was Maurice Hodgens, a local favorite who had gone to Jemison High School. Brother Hodgens was poor like everybody else. He was trying to get through college, but he wasn't very far along. He was very enthusiastic. As he proceeded with a sermon, his voice got louder and louder. Finally, he was shouting, his face red, and the veins in his neck stood out. This got our undivided attention. His words gave a vivid and fearful description of what was in store if we didn't follow his admonitions.

One of the leaders in the Baptist Church was Columbus Conway, a deacon and a successful merchant. At least once each service Mr. Conway was asked to pray, and he would go on for interminable lengths. Mr. Conway was the uncontested champion when it came to long prayers.

I always dreaded a Columbus Conway prayer because he continued far beyond my attention span and my ability to sit quietly with bowed head. One day I noticed that wasps would come out of the attic around the ceiling lights and fly in curious patterns, sometimes coming close to Mr. Conway's head. Watching them helped the time pass during a lengthy prayer and, I discovered, during a long-winded sermon. They would sometimes dive-bomb the preacher, testing his ability to maintain composure.

Brother Hodgens would sometimes have to be away on Sunday. He was usually replaced by Homer Carroll, another Baptist preacher who lived in Jemison. Brother Carroll was the original man of the woeful countenance. He had a very sad face. He would get carried away with the substance of his message when he preached, and he couldn't get through a sermon without shedding tears. Barbara always said she wanted Brother Carroll to hold her funeral when she died because he was so mournful.

The Methodist church was also over in town. Even though they couldn't afford a preacher, they made sure their youngsters had the proper spin on things through their Sunday School. After Sunday School everyone would go to the Baptist Church for the 11 a.m. service. This was a nice gesture, and the Baptists returned the favor by supporting the Methodists when they had a revival.

The only hitch was that every six months or so, the Baptists had communion. The preacher explained as best he could that Baptists believed only members of the Baptist Church could take communion there. The preacher tried to make it clear the Methodist should not take this personally, but the Methodists always arose in a body and marched out.

BARBARA AND I STARTED school at Jemison in the fall of 1937. I was in the second grade and Miss Meggs was my teacher. Miss Meggs also boarded at our house. Barbara was in the sixth grade and had Edna Reynolds.

I liked Miss Meggs, and I liked school. Second grade was a lot of fun. One time we were throwing spit balls, and I got out of my seat to retrieve one when I thought Miss Meggs wasn't looking. My head was under the next desk, and my bottom was sticking up. Miss Meggs gave me a hard swat on it and changed my attitude about spit ball throwing, at least for the day.

Barbara wasn't quiet as enamored with Mrs. Reynolds. Even though Mother thought Mrs. Reynolds was very nice, Barbara insisted the reputation spread by the other students had to be correct. The students told Barbara Mrs. Reynolds was mean to everybody, made the class listen to what she was teaching, and certainly would not put up with any foolishness. If someone acted up, she really got him. The other teachers had pets, but not Mrs. Reynolds! Mother countered by telling Barbara that Mrs. Reynolds might be tough, but she was just doing her job; Barbara was in school to learn.

Jemison had grades one through twelve on a single campus. It was consolidated and served the north end of the county. The largest of the school's three buildings had ten classrooms and an auditorium. A smaller four-room building housed the first and second grades, and a large metal building served as a gymnasium during the school year and a storage location for school bus bodies during the summer.

Our neighbor, James Albert Peterson, was the principal. He was a small, mild-mannered man and was mentally as tough as nails. He became principal in 1924, after teaching chemistry a few years at Chilton County High School in Clanton. Mr. Peterson was fair. He backed his teachers and would stand up to anybody. Rough and tough parents came in from time to time to have it out with him. These parents made their living through manual labor and could have whipped him easily in a fight. Threaten as they might, Mr. Peterson never backed down, and nobody ever had the nerve to strike him. He was universally respected.

JUNIOR SOON BECAME MY best friend. I saw him almost every day during summer. Junior was a grade ahead of me, so I mostly saw him on weekends when school was in session. First and second grades were in a separate building and had recess at different times.

Junior would come to my house or I would go to his. Activities in the Hayman house didn't get much supervision because Mother was in the cafe most of the time. This meant that we could run around and bang on the piano and such without being fussed at.

When the weather was nice, we played in the lumber yard. It was really fun. We could move the boards around on the lumber stacks and make about any type of structure we wanted, such as houses, castles, saloons, hotels, and trains. The saw dust pile was good for building landscapes, and we could run and jump and fall without being hurt.

One day Junior came in the cafe very excited. He had been given five small ducks by some of his country cousins. As the ducks grew, they organized their own social order, and the most handsome one, Quack Quack, emerged as leader. The ducks would walk around in a line with Quack Quack at the head. Junior's yard had plenty of space, food, and a little pond. But the ducks liked our barnyard. In spite of everything Junior could do, Quack Quack led them regularly across the highway

Several times Mother told Junior to keep his ducks out of our barnyard. They bothered the cows and irritated the chickens. Besides, it was dangerous when they crossed the highway. Junior insisted he was trying as hard as he could to keep the ducks at home. He decided he might build a fence.

One day it had been raining, and Junior came in the cafe sobbing. He informed us that there was a water puddle in the middle of the road. Quack Quack started over to our side, and when he came to the puddle, he sat down. The other ducks waited in line behind him. A car came flying around the curve and killed them all. Oh, boo-hoo!

Junior would do one thing on Saturday afternoons that I just couldn't understand. He would listen to the Metropolitan Opera on the radio. I was used to Bob Wills, Roy Acuff, and Ernest Tubb. That opera stuff had the strangest sound.

I asked Junior why he liked that stuff. It sounded screechy to me. He told me that it was all an accident. It seemed that one Saturday while turning the dial on the radio, he discovered a broadcast of the Metropolitan Opera. He listened, liked it, and had been listening ever since. He certainly had broken from the tradition of the Grand Ole Opry. I just shrugged my shoulders and tried not to show my ignorance.

One day I went to Junior's house, and I could tell he had been crying. I asked him what was wrong. At first he just cried and wouldn't tell me. I suppose the pressure inside was building up too rapidly and he knew he would explode if he didn't share his sorrow. I was to hear about a world unknown to me.

I knew that Junior's parents were divorced, and while I found that kind of puzzling, I didn't think a lot about it. To me, Junior was just my friend who lived across the street.

Apparently, Big Marvin—as everyone called Junior's dad—would not bring the monthly child support check willingly. Marvin's mother had to go get it. Rather than facing her ex, she sent Junior, hoping some mercy would be shown. Unfortunately, that was not the case. Big Marvin would rant and rave and would make degrading comments about Mrs. Dawson. Big Marvin apparently did not realize the current nor the long-term impact this had on his son.

BILL DUBOSE CAME IN the cafe at least once every day. Bill was widely read. He kept up with local and national events, and he was a good talker. We all liked Bill a lot.

Bill had an embarrassment, however. He worked hard projecting himself as a man of the world, but his father was a Holiness preacher. Preacher Dubose was a widower and had two sets of children—one set older and one set younger. The older children were members of the Holiness church and were very religious. They lived in south Alabama. The younger ones, Bill, Rebecca, and Jimmie Ruth, lived in Jemison and didn't attend the

Holiness church. Jimmie Ruth was one of Barbara's close friends.

Brother Dubose preached regularly in Clanton, and he also went vary-ing places and plied his trade with tent revivals. He even "tented" in the lumber yard across the street. He survived on whatever offerings people had to give him.

At night there was much shouting and foot-stomping and swooning, and it was a grand spectacle. Brother Dubose would ask one of the local girls, Doris Guy, to play the piano. Doris was really good with boogie-woogie. She played this style for the revival, and her music contributed greatly to the general spirit of things. The meeting lasted a week. We would observe from the front porch of the house or go over and sit on the back bench in the tent.

Bill was mortified. He was trying to be sophisticated, and here was his daddy undermining all of his efforts. While Brother Dubose gave his fire and brimstone sermon in a voice which could be heard in Thorsby three miles south, Bill would stride back and forth in the cafe in great distress.

AFTER A YEAR OR SO, the cafe had become a favorite meeting place. Mother had a good personality and liked to have fun. The cafe was always neat, and there was never the slightest hint of anything untoward. Parents were more than happy to have their children there.

Good food was served at a good price. The vegetables were good because they were fresh. Dad decided early on that one of his contributions would be a large vegetable garden. It was on a couple of acres behind the barn. The main idea was to save money. An added benefit was that the fresh garden produce made our food taste better than the competition.

The garden had turnip greens, collard greens, okra, tomatoes, peas, beans, onions, corn, potatoes, cabbage, lettuce, and other good things. Each day Mother decided what vegetables she would serve, and Dad would go to the garden and gather them. The vegetables would be washed and ready in time for the noon meal. Dad spent a good part of the remainder of the day working in his garden.

Dad thought it would be good if I worked in the garden, too. From the time I was about nine years old, he had me helping. He felt this activity would help me contribute to our livelihood and teach me responsibility and the virtues of hard work. I felt there must be an easier way to accomplish these goals because hoeing made my back hurt, the okra fuzz stung, and I hated picking the worms off the beans. I became an expert in figuring out ways to avoid garden work. This was the time when the thoughts of going to college blossomed seriously in my head.

DAD AND MOTHER ALSO figured that raising our own beef would help. We had a pasture of about five acres which ran along the ditch and stretched from the barnyard to the back of our property. Dad soon had five or six cows. He and Jack would milk them morning and night, and the milk and butter were used or sold in the cafe. Occasionally, a cow would be butchered and the meat stored at Chilton Quick Freeze in Clanton.

We also had chickens and kept a pig or two. This kept the cafe expenses down and helped us keep solvent. Other people started restaurants, but they didn't last long. They had to buy all of their supplies, and their food often wasn't very fresh.

I became well acquainted with the animals, and I felt sad when one of them paid the supreme price to help keep the business profitable. I didn't feel this way about the chickens. When Mother was ready to cook one, she surveyed the flock and picked her victim. She would grab it by the head and, holding the head in her hand, crank it like she was trying to start a Model-T Ford. After a little jerk, the head snapped off and the body would flop around. Watching this fiasco destroyed my appetite for chicken forevermore.

I NOTICED THAT CERTAIN men liked to come and talk with Dad. He didn't stay in the garden and the field all of the time. Sometimes it rained. Sometimes he had everything caught up, and in winter there wasn't a lot to do. Dad sat in the back booth next to the kitchen, and people such as Mr. Pitts, a lawyer from Clanton, would come by and talk a while. I questioned Mother about why folks wanted to talk to my Dad. I didn't think he had that much to talk about. Mother told me that Dad was very smart and read a lot.

I continued my questioning, "If Dad is so smart why doesn't he run the cafe? Why does he let you do it?"

"He does a lot more than you realize," Mother answered. "I cook the food and meet the people, but I talk with him every night about our business. He advises me on the decisions I have to make, and I follow his suggestions. I couldn't run it without him."

Bill Dubose was smart, too. I liked Bill, and when he and Dad were talking, I would ease up and listen. Their conversation covered many things. Someone said that the three major topics of conversation are sex, religion, and politics. I heard them talk a lot about politics and world affairs and some about religion. I didn't hear a word about sex. I guess they held that until they were sure I wasn't around.

Bill talked about possible inventions with Dad. Bill's mind was very fertile, and the ideas poured out. Dad's role was to help separate the wheat from the chaff and play the devil's advocate. I remember such ideas as a new stanchion to handle cows when a person wanted to milk them, a football helmet which would protect the brain, and a system for cooling a room in the hot Alabama summer. All of this seemed marvelous to me, and I wondered how I could get Bill to let me be his assistant.

I asked Bill from time to time if I could work with him, and he always answered, "You'd really be good help. But you need to grow a little more. Maybe when you get bigger and older, you can help." I thought this was the typical adult talk.

As things became busier with the cafe, Mother sometimes needed extra help in the front. She had been thinking about it, but she hadn't hired anyone. One day Bill Dubose allowed as how things were a little slow in the inventing business, and he needed some extra cash. He asked Mother if he could wait tables from time to time. She agreed and set a precedent of having young men as cafe help.

The Depression was still on, and many men in their twenties and thirties around Jemison didn't have jobs. They lived with their parents. Nobody thought much about it because times were like this all over the country.

One of our favorite helpers was Glen Green. He made fancy signs for the cafe. One said, "Milk, 5 cents a pint," with large, unusual letters.

Glen's dad was a preacher. Glen's brother Guy was married to Geraldine

Bean, and because times were so hard, Geraldine and Guy lived with their respective parents.

One day, Geraldine talked to Mother about giving her brother, James Lloyd Bean, a job. Mother hired him as a regular employee. He became one of our favorites. James Lloyd was in senior high. It didn't take long for Barbara to develop a crush on James Lloyd, but to her disdain, he did not reciprocate.

Everybody called James Lloyd "Puny." I was still a little twerp, and I couldn't figure out why they called him Puny. He looked pretty big to me.

IN THOSE DAYS, THE ambulance and the hearse were the same vehicle. If someone was hurt in a wreck or sick and needed fast transportation, the funeral home in Clanton was called. The ambulance drivers often stopped for a cup of coffee when they were in the northern part of the county. I was fascinated by their vehicle and always ran out when they drove up. The driver would give me a thrill by pulling a little switch out and pushing it back in, causing the siren to squeal. I watched this several times and thought the switch had to be pumped to make it siren.

One day the drivers pulled in beside the cafe and went in. I got into the ambulance and decided I would experiment. I pulled out the switch, and the siren started. Instead of pushing the switch back in, I jumped out of the ambulance and ran. The driver had to shut it off. It didn't do any harm, but I was terribly embarrassed. Everyone had a big laugh over my dumb caper. I was mortified.

THE COUNTY HEALTH DEPARTMENT gave free shots in Jemison from time to time. Typhoid fever shots were offered every summer. The first time a person was vaccinated for typhoid, a shot was taken each week for three consecutive weeks. After that, a booster shot was given each year. The health people usually used the ground floor of the Masonic Hall for their work, but one summer they decided to give the shots in the cafe. I thought that was great! I knew Mother was going to have me take the shots, so I said to Mother, "I want to be first when they give the shots. I'm going to march right up there and be brave."

"That's fine," she said.

I went around bragging to everyone who came in, "I'm going to be first in line for the shots so I can show how to do it."

When the day for the first shots came, the health people arrived and started setting up their equipment. They had a Bunsen burner and alcohol, and it smelled like a doctor's office. As I watched them lay the needles out, my heart sank, and my nerve completely left me just as they were ready to start.

Mother said, "Well, John, go to the head of the line and show us how brave you are."

I wouldn't go. Finally someone else went first, and I sneaked to the back. I could see what was happening, and I decided I didn't want any shot at all. Mother thought otherwise, so when she couldn't persuade me to go voluntarily, she dragged me up there.

I cried and kicked and screamed, and it took Mother and a couple of the health people to hold me and administer the shot. I was terribly humiliated. I made a complete fool of myself in front of a room full of people, all of whom had heard me brag. They thought it was pretty funny. I decided maybe pride doth go before a fall!

4

We didn't talk a lot about sports when we first moved to Jemison. Back in Arkansas, Dad had been a big baseball fan. I remember him going occasionally with some other men to Little Rock to see the Travelers play or to Memphis to see the Chicks. Both were in the Southern Association.

He didn't get into it after we moved to Alabama. The Birmingham Barons were in the same league, but Dad was having trouble with his health and was worried about his job. In Jemison, Mother and Dad had more basic concerns than baseball.

I thought about it, though. Before I got run over, I figured it was just a short time before I would be a baseball player. Baseball was something the big boys did, and I thought I would reach that status in just a year or two. I talked about it with my friends. They agreed we were on the verge of being big, so they planned to play, too. After we moved to Jemison, I figured the time would be there as soon as my leg healed.

I wanted to play for the St. Louis Cardinals, and I wanted to be just like Dizzy Dean. In Brasfield everybody talked about the Cardinals and listened to them on the radio. My friends and I had great times pretending we were Dizzy Dean. We thought he must be something else to have a name like that. We would get out in the dirt road in front of our house and would yell, "Dizzy Dean, Dizzy Dean," while turning around and around until we were dizzy and fell over. This was all accompanied by great laughter. So I had Dizzy Dean and the Cardinals planted in my head.

In Jemison, people didn't seem to talk as much about baseball. As the cafe became the social center of town, the customers gathered there to talk about basketball, especially during the fall and winter months. We had never had any interest in basketball, so we were pretty dumb about it.

Bill Dubose would talk about the games up at the school. When he brought the teachers in, they would discuss it at great length. They would dissect our win over Maplesville or our narrow loss to Clanton. They all seemed very excited. I would hear about Big James hitting a hook shot and Willie getting a crucial basket from the outside.

We soon got the idea that basketball was a special thing in Jemison and maybe we ought to pay more attention to it.

About this time, Coach Zane Turner from the high school started coming in regularly. He was very friendly, and we liked him. Everyone liked to talk with Coach Turner, and it was clear that he was one of the heroes of the town. He would say something to me at times, and I really liked having a grown up pay attention to me—and a hero at that!

So we attended a game in the old metal building at Jemison High School. It was big and lofty, with no interior finish, and it had a dirt floor which had to be oiled to keep the dust down. The only heat was a couple of pot-bellied stoves on each side. It could get really cold in the winter time.

It seemed that everybody in town was at the game. There were some wooden bleachers at the sides, but I could see that people didn't sit very much. I decided that the bleachers were to stand on, and they were built up like that so that you could see over the person in front of you. The atmosphere heated up pretty fast. It might be cold at the start, but everyone was soon jumping up and down and hollering. They forgot all about the outside temperature.

The games were very exciting. Coach Turner *really* wanted to win, and he would get worked up on the sidelines. His coat would come off, and his hair would get ruffled. He would walk back and forth in increasing agitation. He imparted his strong desire to win to his players, and they played very hard. The townspeople wanted to win, too. There was great cheering as the game went on. When Coach yelled at the referee, and this was fairly often, everybody on the sidelines took up the cause. Everyone was in it together.

We were hooked right away. We went to all of the games, got excited, and cheered just like everybody else.

When the game neared its end, we would edge toward the door, and as soon as the final whistle blew we would rush to the cafe. Mother would open up, and everybody who had been at the game would come in to have a cold drink (cola) and a hamburger and to relive the excitement. In a few minutes, Coach Turner and the basketball players would come in.

It was really fun. Everybody would have a marvelous time for an hour or so laughing and talking about the game. Most of the players lived in the country, and none of them had access to a car. No high school student had a car, and few of their parents had one. The players needed a ride home, and after their stop at the cafe, Coach would drive them home.

The players were all my heroes, and pretty soon I forgot about baseball and Dizzy Dean. What I wanted to be was a basketball player and to play for the Jemison Panthers under Coach Turner. I imagined myself shooting from mid-court with one second left and beating Clanton by one point. How glorious! The players were Barbara's heroes, too. Once when I sneaked and overheard her talking to someone, I learned that she had a crush on one of them! This information came in handy when I was mad about something and wanted to irritate her.

MANY OF THE GOOD basketball players came from Collins Chapel, a community about four miles southeast of Jemison. Collins Chapel's school went through the ninth grade. After finishing there, the students came to high school at Jemison for the last three grades. Collins Chapel had a junior high basketball team, and they were serious about it. They played a regular schedule with other junior high schools and won most of their games. When their boys came to Jemison in the tenth grade, they had already played three or four years.

The Union Grove and Oak Grove communities also had junior high schools which fed into Jemison. Sometimes they would have a good basketball player. Union Grove was east of town, and Oak Grove was north, so Coach had quite a drive when he delivered all of the players home.

We were really into it by the fall of 1938, and Jemison had a talented team. One of the good players was Horace Cleckley, who lived right outside of town. Three of the best players were from Collins Chapel. They were Little Willie Smith, Little James Smith, and Big James Smith. Little Willie was the object of Barbara's crush, but he never knew about it.

Everybody really liked Big James Smith. He played center and was good. Like Coach, Big James was determined to win. He had a hot and quick temper, and the fact that he sometimes let it get out of control added to the excitement. When Big James got mad, his lips would turn purple. We all watched for this sign; when we saw it, we knew the other team had better watch out. Big James was about to get them!

Coach was always lecturing Big James to keep his temper under control and not get in a fight. When the lips turned blue, Coach would sometimes take him out a few minutes to let him cool off. One night we were at a game, and the other team kept playing rough. Coach complained about it several times to the referees but to no avail.

Shortly, Big James' lips started turning blue, and we all knew there was going to be trouble. Before Coach could do anything about it, a player on the other team pushed Big James pretty hard, and Big James let him have it right in the mouth. When Coach went running out to try to stop it, one of the opposing players pushed Coach. Coach lost his temper and started fighting right along with Big James and the rest of his team. The state athletic association didn't think too highly of Coach's behavior, but Jemison folks loved him for it.

COACH TURNER BECAME ONE of our really good friends. He made a regular habit of coming to the cafe on Sunday afternoons. Many of the other townspeople came by, too, and it was a joy for a boy to hear and be a part of it.

As we came to know Coach better, he told us he grew up on a farm in Livingston, the western part of Alabama. He was always attracted to sports and had a dream of attending the University of Alabama. In 1920, he had scraped up enough money to attend. He got excited about football in his freshman year when Xen Scott was the coach, but really became a Crimson Tide fan in 1923, his senior year, when Wallace Wade became coach. It was evident his ardor had not cooled.

After Coach finished at the University, he taught a couple of years around Livingston. At that time, Jemison had Coach Owens. Owens got in a fuss with Mr. Peterson and resigned. Mr. Peterson asked some people at the University to recommend a replacement, and Coach Turner was hired.

Before Coach Turner, Jemison's basketball team was pretty average for a school its size. It didn't take long for things to change. By the early 1930s Jemison was one of the powers in the state.

Coach always said that his very best team was the one he was currently coaching. Bill Dubose would differ, and would brag, "The team of 1934 was the best high school basketball team in the state of Alabama, barring none. We could beat anyone—Clanton, Selma, those big schools in Birmingham."

When I heard they could beat Clanton, my eyes got bigger, and I joined in. "Did they win the state championship?"

"Well, we should have," Coach said. "We won the district tournament in Selma without much trouble, but we lost in the state tournament to the team that eventually became the champion. We should have won that game, but I just didn't coach well enough."

We all sat in silence. Coach Turner was the greatest in the world, and we didn't much like his answer. "That's hard to believe," I thought to myself, but I didn't say anything. Questions about the great Jemison team of 1934 remained in the back of my mind and went unanswered.

It wasn't long before basketball started again, and the folks at school decided to move the games into the school auditorium. It was smaller than a regular-size court, and it had a pretty low ceiling, but we were all getting ashamed of the old tin building with the dirt floor. The auditorium was much nicer, though like the old gym, it had stoves on each side for heat.

On a game day, the boys would move the folding benches into the auditorium. Some benches went on the sidelines and some on the stage, but most were folded and stored away. There were two rows of benches along the sidelines and about three on the stage. People sitting behind the first row on the stage couldn't see very well, so they just stood up. The stage held a pretty good crowd.

It turned out there was a certain advantage to the Jemison team using the auditorium. Our players learned to shoot long shots with a low arch to avoid hitting the ceiling. Teams like Clanton and the Birmingham schools, which had a regular gym, didn't have this skill, so their shots tended to hit the ceiling. This was out of bounds, and Jemison got the ball.

Also, everybody yelled a lot at the games, and they jumped up and down and stomped the floor. All of this noise drifted off into the rafters in the old gym, but in the auditorium, it was concentrated. It cheered our boys on and intimidated the opposition.

There wasn't much space at the side of the court, so Coach had a hard time staying on the sidelines. He was very animated at games, and would stride rapidly back and forth. Sometimes the referees got him—and we got the referees.

The players from the two opposing teams sat close to the stove on each side, more or less in the middle of the court. This put Coach in a dangerous position part of the time. Once, during a tight game, Coach was greatly agitated. Something happened that he didn't like, so he kicked the coal scuttle with mighty force. It broke his foot, and he had to hobble around in a cast for a few weeks. We loved him even more.

LATE ONE SPRING AFTERNOON we were all sitting in the cafe talking. Bill Dubose was there, talking about world affairs with Dad. In walks a nice looking man about Bill's age. He was introduced as a Jemison native who was currently working in Birmingham. His name was Joyce Howard, who just happened to have played on that famous 1934 team. I was rather awed to meet such a one. I thought maybe my previous unanswered questions would finally be resolved. Barbara couldn't stand the suspense either, so she asked him to tell us what happened.

"We were good, and we thought we could beat anybody," Joyce pronounced. "We almost did. We lost in the state tournament by one point to the team which beat everybody else with ease and won the championship. We thought we had beaten them, but the tournament officials took it away from us."

"How did that happen," Barbara asked.

"Well," Joyce answered, "We were playing Scottsboro, and it was a really close game all the way. The lead had gone back and forth several times. Right at the end, Scottsboro was one point ahead. We took the ball to our end of the court, and someone threw it to me. I passed to J. T. Cobb, and J. T. shot a basket. But one of the directors of the tournament said that time had run out before his shot was far enough in the air. If the shot had been allowed, Jemison would have won by one point. We argued as strong as we could, but they gave the game to Scottsboro. The only thing we could do was come on back home and feel sorry for ourselves. But in our hearts we knew we were better than Scottsboro."

It didn't take much prompting for Joyce to recall the names of the team members: "J. T. and I were forwards, Alton Cobb was center and sometimes played forward. John Busby and Cecil Ellison were the guards. We were the starting five. Herbert Watson and John Lowrey were substitutes, but they were also really good.

"I played four years, starting in 1931. We went to the district tournament in Selma every year. We were runners-up in the district tournament in 1933, and we won it in 1934. We went to the state tournament in Tuscaloosa in '33 and '34.

"The team in 1935, the year after I graduated, was good, too. They won the district tournament and were going to go to Tuscaloosa, but someone turned them in for having an ineligible player. Jemison was disqualified, and the district championship was awarded to the runner-up, Maplesville. The ineligible player was my good buddy, J. T. Cobb. He still had a year left in high school after I graduated. He and I played semi-pro baseball in Alexander City that previous summer, and he wasn't supposed to do that. Somebody found out about it and turned him in."

Joyce began to get interested in sports about the eighth grade, he said. His biggest thrill was to go watch the tournament games in Selma, but he had a hard time getting there. He lived out in the country and didn't have any money. His grandmother would catch a chicken or two and give them to him. Joyce would sell them at one of the grocery stores in Jemison and use the money to go to Selma to the tournament. He would catch a ride with someone, and a lot of times spend the night. On one of the Selma trips, it was late at night, and he was broke. Mr. Turner let Joyce sleep with him. It was not easy to be an avid Jemison Panther fan.

After this round of Cokes and reminiscing, Joyce walked out with a spring in his step. I was really impressed, and now I had another hero to admire. Dizzy Dean was fading further into the mist.

BASKETBALL PLAYERS DIDN'T LOSE their interest in the game just because they graduated from high school. Few of them from Jemison had any thoughts of going to college or of playing at a higher level. What they did instead was to play on the "town team."

Every community with a high school also had a town team made up of players who had graduated. They would often play before the regular high school game. We liked them and cheered for them, too, but they didn't excite us as much as the high school team.

The players on the town team couldn't afford to buy uniforms. This problem was solved by local merchants or sometimes by companies which sold things in Jemison. Each contributor bought one uniform, and his identification was printed on it. The uniforms had numbers like the high school uniforms, but they also said things like "Bratton's Store," "Martha White Flour," and "Royster Fertilizer."

BASKETBALL WASN'T THE ONLY sport played in Jemison. We didn't have a football team, but there was baseball in the spring and summer. In the spring, the high school played, and in the summer it was the town team, whose uniforms also carried company names. We pulled for our baseball teams to win, but with modest enthusiasm.

Beating Clanton was fun any time, and the high school baseball team did it in 1939. The hero was the shortstop, James Littlejohn. Twice during the game, James came to bat with Henry Sims on second base and Princeton Simmons on third. Both times James hit a double over the left fielder's head into a thorn thicket. The final score was Jemison 7, Clanton 0. We all celebrated.

James, Henry, Princeton, and several other boys also played on the town team in the summer. James' brother Charles played first base, and the catcher was Murray Glass, whose father owned a large flat-bed truck. Murray would drive the truck to out-of-town games, and the players and anyone else who wanted to go would ride along. The truck bed was usually full, and I loved being on there with everyone else. It was sort of like riding Columbus Conway's truck to church picnics or the state fair.

The town team players liked to practice, and I liked to watch them. One day I noticed that the ball they were using did not have any visible seams.

That night James Littlejohn came in the cafe. "Where did y'all get that baseball you were playing with this afternoon?" I asked.

"Uncle Henry Conway makes them in his filling station over in town," James answered. "If it weren't for him we couldn't play because nobody has enough money to buy baseballs. Uncle Henry gets a little rubber ball and winds twine around it. Then he wraps white tape all around the outside. They work real good. If you'll notice, we use them in the games, too."

"Who do y'all play next?" I asked.

"Mars Hill is coming over here Saturday," he said. "It'll be a good game. They have a left-handed pitcher who just drives us crazy. His name is Lefty Cofer. He can take Uncle Henry's wound tape ball and do all kinds of things with it."

I thought to myself, "I bet Dizzy Dean could do a lot more."

COACH TURNER'S POPULARITY DIDN'T fade. As customary in most high schools, Coach also taught. He taught science, and he was good at that, too. Barbara had Coach as homeroom teacher in the ninth grade.

Years later when I was a student at the University of Alabama, I attended summer school. It was a better choice, I figured, than plowing Kit or working in the garden. Many teachers were there working to get to the next step on the salary schedule. Sometimes I would sit with them in the cafeteria. Often, when I told them I was from Jemison, they would exclaim, "That's the school that used to have such good basketball teams!" Though I didn't play, I could not keep my chest from puffing out.

5

Junior and I were sitting on the rock wall in front of our house one afternoon. We were watching Donald Jones direct cars to the office of a black herb doctor who had set up shop a mile or two west of town. The man called himself "Dr. Chapel," and so did the people in town, though everyone knew his doctorate was self-awarded. Cars were coming from everywhere, but, as far as we knew, he had no patients from Jemison.

We didn't know how the people in the cars knew Dr. Chapel was in Jemison, but they did. They just didn't know where in Jemison he was located, so Dr. Chapel paid Donald Jones to stand on U.S. Highway 31 to direct them. Donald didn't work for the doctor full time. He supplemented his job with a rolling cafe he parked by Chapel's office when there was a big crowd. Donald's cafe was built on the bed of a truck.

Junior and I discussed the actual healing powers of Dr. Chapel: whether he was a herb healer or not; how he got people to come to him; and, how he got them to pay for his services. Dr. Chapel's reward was a nice home and the monies to pay Donald Jones. Dr. Chapel's business was short lived, however. It wasn't long before we heard that the health department was after Dr. Chapel and that he had tax problems.

About that time, we noticed someone was moving into a little room on the side of one of Sam Reynolds' stores. We learned that the man, Andrew Price, was setting up an office and that he had moved his family into a rented house on the west side of town. In a day or two, Andrew put up a sign Raymond Reynolds had painted for him. It said, "Dr. Kamp, Herb Specialist."

Dr. Kamp didn't have any patients at first, but he had put his office just a short distance from the intersection where Donald Jones was directing traffic. Pretty soon we noticed that Donald was sending the cars to Dr. Kamp instead of the west side of town. Dr. Kamp's practice picked up fast.

In a short while, the health department really clamped down on Dr. Chapel. He was out of business in a hurry, but Jemison was still host to a herb doctor.

Sometimes Andrew Price would come to the cafe for lunch. He was a short, rather plump, dark-complexioned man who was very friendly and laughed a lot. We all liked him. Mother was curious and started asking questions. She found out that Dr. Kamp (Andrew Price) was basically a local, moving to Jemison from Plantersville, just across the line in Dallas County. It seems he used to have a practice there, too.

Later that afternoon Bill Dubose cracked, "I expect Jemison was a better place for him because that Chapel guy already had a bunch of people driving in. Why do you suppose Donald Jones started directing them the other way?"

I didn't know, but it sounded mighty suspicious. The regular cafe bunch figured Bill was onto the truth, but to the best of my knowledge, nobody ever asked Donald Jones.

ANDREW PRICE HAD FOUR children about our ages. Bruce was the oldest, and soon he was buddies with Junior and me. He had a brother, Llewellyn, and two sisters, Gwendolyn and Barbara Jean. Gwendolyn was a real looker, a fact soon noticed by the older boys.

After we became better acquainted, Junior asked Bruce, "Why does the sign say 'Dr. Kamp' when your daddy's name is Price? Ain't that confusing to the people who come to see him?" We'd all been curious about that.

"It wasn't supposed to say Dr. Kamp," Bruce explained. "It was supposed to say, 'Doctor's Camp,' but Raymond Reynolds misunderstood. Raymond painted two signs, one for each side of the chinaberry tree, but he didn't show them to Daddy until they were finished. They looked so good, Daddy just let it go. Some people call him Dr. Kamp, and some call him Dr. Price. I don't guess it matters as long as they know where to find him."

BUSINESS PICKED UP VERY fast for Andrew, and soon he was doing better than Chapel ever dreamed of. It was clear that he had something special. To add a little mystery, he told his patients that he was part American Indian.

People in town learned about it and had great fun with biting remarks. They knew he had moved from the next county and had about as much Indian blood as the rest of us.

Andrew wanted to verify his claim of being part-Indian, at least with outsiders who came to see him. Some transient Indians came along one day, and Andrew hired them to put on their costumes, parade up and down in front of his office, and call him "Cousin Wahoo." The Indians left, but the name "Wahoo" stuck. He preferred to be known as Dr. Price, but from that point forward, he was Wahoo to everyone in Jemison.

Our family started calling him Wahoo behind his back like everybody else, even though we liked him. We had special reason to be grateful to him. His patients had to eat somewhere, and Donald Jones was now digging herbs in the woods instead of operating his rolling cafe. The cafe wouldn't have fit on the side of the highway anyway. As Wahoo's business picked up, so did ours. By late 1939, the year after the Prices moved to Jemison, the cafe was doing a good bit better than just subsistence level.

It was a very good year for Andrew Price. He bought the house the family had been renting. The room on the side of Sam Reynolds' building was far too small by then, so Andrew bought a larger building across the street from us. He had it fixed up with a nice office and waiting room, and he improved the parking area in front. Also, about four miles east of Jemison, he bought Mineral Springs Sanitarium, an old resort known for its mineral water.

Andrew did some remodeling at Mineral Springs, and he made opening day at the new facility a grand event. He had a big barbecue, and he brought in a famous radio preacher, C. C. Wilcox, to help with the entertainment. Everybody was curious about the remodeled building, and barbecue would be a treat. There would have been a big crowd just with that. But Preacher Wilcox was the *piece de resistance*. A big throng showed up to see the famous man, and they bought a lot of barbecue.

Junior and I asked Bruce if they made any money that day.

"Yep. Daddy was really happy," Bruce answered. "He charged $1.10 a plate for the barbecue. That's a lot, but they all wanted to see the preacher. Daddy had him spread things out over several hours. I overheard Daddy tell Mom that they almost took in enough to pay for the place."

Andrew (Wahoo) had purchased Mineral Springs from Tom Hand, who had purchased the place in 1933. There had been a resort hotel on the hill above the spring before World War I. It was a two-story building made of wood, and it had a porch that ran all around the top floor. Mr. Hand had the idea of using it for a health resort. He built a one-story building just below the spring. A gravity fed water system was put in so that water from the spring went through faucets, baths, and flush toilets. Mr. Hand put in generators for electricity. But Mr. Hand was getting old, the Depression was underway, and there weren't enough people with money to visit a resort. Mr. Hand figured he could never finish what he started. So Andrew purchased the property thinking it would be a good place to enlarge his business. He added another story and made changes so it would be more like a hospital.

Two artificial lakes had been built below the building. I asked what they were for. Bruce said, "They're just there to make it look peaceful. Dad wants people to be able to rest and relax while they're here."

ANDREW PRICE WAS MAKING a big success of things, and interest in him and his activities picked up among the town folks. Rumors began to circulate about the way he handled patients.

Bill Dubose told us that Wahoo's method was carefully calculated to make the patient believe. "When they enter his office," Bill explained, "the patient sits in front of a desk facing the good doctor. He gives them a long steady look straight in the eyes. He carefully examines their fingernails. Finally, he puts his head in his hands and goes into what appears to be a trance. After a minute or two he relates the patient's medical history. He tells where they hurt, any operations they have had, how they generally feel, and their history of illnesses. He then pronounces with great authority, 'I can cure you.'"

Bill continued, "This is followed by prescriptions of herbs, different mixtures of liquids, and a couple of jugs of mineral water. The patient apparently believes some mysterious process handed down through Indian lore is at work, and most of them believe that their cure is imminent. They sit a little straighter and begin to feel better even before they have a taste of the medicine."

Bill thought he knew part of the secret of success. "Large containers of Epsom Salts come into the depot for him," he said, "and almost any of us would feel better with the kind of workout that provides. Also, I've heard that Four Roses is included in some of the prescriptions."

We all turned serious at Bill's last sentence. Four Roses was a leading brand of whiskey, and Chilton County was strictly dry. We knew from our Southern Baptist teachings that no self-respecting person would even think of taking a drink of an alcoholic beverage.

Mother questioned Bill about the use of herbs. "The right herbs can be good for you," Bill declared. "The Indians used them all the time, and so do people in other parts of the world. I don't know how much Wahoo really knows, but he's got Donald Jones digging herbs in the woods, and someone'd better be watching that pretty close."

"We're beginning to hear these outlandish claims of people being cured by Wahoo," Mother said. "Do you think they're true?"

"Well," Bill replied. "I've always heard that a requirement for any cure is to believe you're going to get better. Wahoo gets them believing, then when the Epsom Salts makes them feel better, it reinforces their thinking. I guess you could say that they cure themselves. But that's okay. The Good Book says if you have enough faith, you can do anything."

Even so, the Jemison folks did not visit Wahoo for healing. They thought he was a fake and had no faith in him. I thought Bill's was the most ingenious explanation. My admiration for Bill's mental powers increased significantly. I started paying close attention to what Wahoo's patients in the cafe said about him. One thing was for sure—they all believed in him.

We continued to be fascinated by the growing crowds across the street and by the growing prosperity of the Price family. Fascination or not, we remained suspicious of Wahoo's abilities as a healer, and appalled by the rumor that he had an eye for the girls. The rumors resulted in many tsks of disapproval.

As THE WEATHER COOLED off that fall, I came down with a good case of the flu. I had to stay home from school, which I really didn't mind, but I felt pretty bad, which I did mind.

Dad tried doctoring me with his favorite medicinal concoction, a toddy with a shot of whiskey and some lemon juice in a glass of hot water. Dad was one of the few people in Chilton County who could legally own a bottle of whiskey—a prescription, given by the doctor as a stimulant for his heart. Because it was medicine, it didn't fall under the Southern Baptist moral code. His concoction worked wonders. It didn't change my physical condition so much as the awful taste made me determined to improve as fast as I could.

To ease things, Dad took a couple of hours each afternoon to read *David Copperfield* to me. He read slowly and stopped from time to time to ask me what I thought of something in the story. At first I thought this was going to be boring. The book looked so thick, and Dad wasn't one for foolishness. But soon I was into it and couldn't wait for the session to begin. Dad surprised me. He was a good reader, and he was very patient.

I stayed sick long enough for Dad to go completely through the book. I felt pretty good the last two hundred pages, but I wanted to hear the rest of it. Also, I wasn't anxious to get back to school. I think Dad suspected I really didn't need to stay home anymore, but he was enjoying our sessions, too. So we had a little conspiracy going. I learned from this experience that, although my Dad wasn't very good at expressing affection verbally, he really was a caring person, and he cared more for me than I had realized.

About a week after I recovered from the flu, Dad told me he wanted to discuss something with me privately. I couldn't imagine what we needed to talk about, but I went with him to sit in the swing on the front porch of the house. The subject of our discussion was "The Facts of Life." Our reading sessions together convinced him that I was old enough to "know the truth." I was puzzled, but I sat silently waiting to hear the truth about something I wasn't much concerned about. Dad made a fumbling attempt to explain how all this worked, but he struggled. I knew the Bible taught that we were made from dust, but I didn't understand Dad's dialogue on how the dust of the earth was changed into a baby. Finally Dad asked if I understood what he was telling me. Feeling a bit embarrassed, I told him I thought so, but underneath I was disappointed that he hadn't gone into more detail. I wanted to know more, but I could see that Dad was uneasy with his task, and I didn't have enough nerve to pursue it.

I pondered the next few months how the box of dirt could be changed into a baby. Finally, some boys at school informed me that my vision was incorrect. They talked and joked about sex, using some words that I could tell should not be repeated at home. Even with their explanation, I was as mystified about sex as I was about the box of dirt.

ONE SATURDAY AFTERNOON THAT fall, Junior, Bruce Price, and I were sitting on a lumber stack across from the cafe. We each had a cold drink and were discussing the mysteries of life, such as we understood them. One of our mysteries was how people get money. Neither Bruce nor I knew how to earn any. Junior surprised us with the pronouncement that he was trying by picking cotton. Bruce and I looked at each other in disbelief and suspicion. "Where did you pick cotton?" Bruce asked.

"I picked for Jimbo East," Junior exclaimed. "He has a big patch, and I heard he needed help. So I asked him. He said he doubted I was big enough to do any good, but if I wanted to, he would let me try. It was last Monday. Golly, it was a hot. A bunch of us were out there, and we were strung out a pretty good ways picking cotton. Well, Jimbo's wife, Viola, was out there, too. She's big and fat, you know, and she was picking away. She's a tough lady. I thought, 'If she can do this, I can too.' My plan was to pick cotton for days and days and make lots of money. At the end of that day, I had earned twenty cents. I could see I wasn't going to get rich. One day did it for me!"

"Well, the Easts must make good money doing it," Bruce observed. "They keep their house going, and it seems to me their daughter dresses kinda pretty."

"They do some funny things," Junior said. "Did you know that Ellie May goes out on her back porch to take a bath? She draws the water from a well on the back porch, heats it up, and takes her bath right there. Everybody in the neighborhood looks. I know she does it on purpose. She's showing everybody what she has, and they all think it's real interesting."

Bruce and I wanted to know the time this event occurred so that we could verify it for ourselves. If I could see that, maybe I could get a little further in understanding the process of using a dirt box to make babies. Junior wouldn't say anything else. He had us going, and he knew when to stop.

THE SCHOOL YEAR MOVED along, the holiday season came and went, Wahoo kept getting more patients, and we became more and more a part of the town. Mother liked to laugh and joke, and she kept a happy atmosphere, even though she wouldn't put up with any foolishness, like cussing or alcohol in the cafe.

As April approached, Mother got a great idea. For April Fool's Day, she went to Woodley's grocery and carefully picked out a sack full of little onions about the size of marbles. The night of March 31, she cooked up a chocolate glaze and dipped the onions in it. After they dried, they looked exactly like candy.

April 1 dawned, and the first person who came in after the breakfast rush was Miss Nancy Wells. Miss Nancy lived about a half block away on the road to town. She was a widow in her late sixties and was one of the "town characters." She was jolly most of the time. When she laughed, which was often, she went "Har, har, har" in kind of a nasal tone that resembled the laugh of Abner on the radio show *Lum and Abner*. She had run the cafe in the early '30s.

Miss Nancy sat at the center table. A little bowl full of the chocolate-covered onions sat on the counter. Mother moved it to the table where Miss Nancy sat and said, "Have some candy, Miss Nancy."

Miss Nancy took one and chomped down on it. Her eyes opened wide in surprise, and in a second or two, she realized what had happened.

"April Fool!" Mother cried.

Miss Nancy doubled over in laughter. "Har, har, har, har, wheeze . . . har, har, har." The walls shook as her merriment grew. Finally she got herself under control. "This is the greatest trick I ever saw," she exclaimed. "I'm going to help you put this one over." She finished her coffee as quickly as she could and headed across the railroad for town. All day long she told people that Mother had made some great candy, and they ought to go over to the cafe and have a piece. A considerable number did.

It was a marvelous prank that solidified Mother's position as one of the really lovable people in Jemison. Everyone shared the surprise and joy, and the awareness grew in their subconscious that the cafe was a place of comfort and cheer where one could forget the Depression and other woes.

The next year Mother pulled another one. She made some little individual pies with a crust and meringue. The surprise was a cotton filling. People would bite into them, then they couldn't get the pie to let go in their mouth. Their first expression of surprise and puzzlement turned into consternation as they struggled to make the pie do what they expected, then the realization that they had been had. Everyone took it in the best of spirits.

Mother had me take one of the pies to Miss Meggs when I returned to school after lunch. Miss Meggs had been my second grade teacher and had boarded with us two years. She had the usual reaction. She decided it was too good a joke to end with her. She fixed the pie to look as if it hadn't been touched and had me take it to her rather plump colleague in the next room. The colleague all but drooled as she eyed the morsel, and she took a big bite. At first, being a sensitive soul and a little touchy about her physique, she thought maybe she should be insulted. An uncertain moment passed. Then great laughter exploded.

LATER THE AFTERNOON OF the chocolate onion April Fool, I gave my teacher a little surprise which she didn't consider very funny. She was Miss Jesse Mims, a good teacher but rather stern and structured in her ways.

When you felt the urge, you raised your hand and asked, "May I be excused?" Normally you were granted this request, but some people abused the privilege. The older boys would sometimes slip around behind the privy and smoke, while the younger ones would just dally around, happy to be free from the classroom for a moment.

The need came upon me. I raised my hand, and when Miss Mims recognized me, I asked, "May I be excused?" It was only a few minutes until afternoon recess, and Miss Mims was in the middle of her spelling lesson, a task she considered very important.

"Please wait a little while," she said.

The urgency grew, and I could see I might not make it until recess. So I raised my hand again. She looked at me sternly.

"I need to be excused, please ma'am."

Somehow she took this as a challenge to her authority, and she answered, "No," in a firm, no-nonsense manner.

The urge was now very strong, and soon it was more than I could control in spite of my best efforts. My underwear and short pants got thoroughly soaked, and a little puddle dripped on the floor.

When Miss Mims glanced my way and saw what happened, her face turned red, and she had to struggle to maintain control. She didn't know what to do next, so she just fumbled around with something on her desk until the bell rang. Her spelling lesson was completely destroyed.

I was terribly humiliated and embarrassed. I sat in my desk trying to hide what had happened as the other kids went out to recess, but the puddle on the floor was visible and unmistakable. They all giggled, making my misery complete. I knew I would be the butt of jokes for a while—"Johnny wet his pants. Johnny wet his pants."

When all the kids had gone out, Miss Mims came over and dried up the puddle with a rag. She sent me home for the rest of the afternoon because my clothes were in such a mess. She didn't say much. I think she wasn't sure if it was an accident or if I did it to spite her. But one thing was for sure, Miss Mims never refused my request again.

WAHOO SELDOM CAME TO the cafe anymore. He was too busy. Every now and then he would slip over for a cup of coffee, and he always laughed and joked. He had plenty to be happy about.

What happened across the street was unbelievable. His patient load kept growing. Soon he had such crowds that he couldn't see them all in one day, and they had to stay overnight in a tourist court in Thorsby or Clanton. He was especially busy on weekends.

People registered in the front office of his building when they arrived, and he took them in order. There were so many that parking became a problem. We would see cars from surrounding states, and occasionally there would be one from some far-off place like Iowa or Oklahoma.

We were mystified as to why all this was happening, and Wahoo's expanding popularity became a subject of much speculation. Apparently word of mouth spread farther and quicker than any of us could imagine. Regardless of the mystery, I was just proud that he was putting Jemison on the map. We had something big that no one else had—not even Clanton!

Junior, Bruce, and I hung out together, and Junior was getting to be friends with Gwendolyn. This prompted the rest of us to kid him about having a sweetie. He didn't deny it. We thought Junior might have learned the secret to Wahoo's success, but if he did, he didn't share it with us.

The Price kids fit right into things in Jemison, and Gwendolyn was becoming popular at school. She was very pretty, kind, and friendly. Junior and Gwendolyn were in the same class in elementary school, and their classmates always voted them king and queen candidates for Valentines. Each class selected candidates, and the overall winner was determined by the number of votes received. Votes were purchased for one cent each at the event.

Junior and Gwendolyn always won the big contest because Wahoo would buy enough votes to make sure of it. After one such occasion, I was kidding Junior about his being the King of Jemison School, the most popular boy in town. He admitted it wasn't because of his popularity, but because of Wahoo's money.

THE SCHOOL YEAR ENDED on the upbeat. I had recovered my dignity after the incident with Miss Mims and was looking forward to fourth grade, with a really pretty teacher named Dotty Brown. The Depression had eased a little, and people were not quite so desperate about their finances. Almost everybody felt good about life, though I could hear the adults talking in worried tones about somebody in Germany named Hitler. The phenomenon across the street had taken us to minor affluence, and the restrictions on candy bars, ice cream, and cold drinks were removed from Barbara and me.

Things were a little better for Junior, too. His mother got a job at Mr. Levine's dry goods store in Clanton. The Levines were Jewish, and so far as I knew, they were the only Jews in Chilton County. Jews were very mysterious to me. I heard about them in church, and thought they were strange people living somewhere else, like the Arabs and Chinese. I soon discovered they were no different than the rest of us.

Jemison was now our home, completely and totally, and as Mother often put it, the Jemison Cafe was our best friend.

6

Barbara and I were sitting in the cafe one spring day. Mother had just received a letter from Uncle Buddy, her brother who lived in Arkansas. She read the letter and then informed us that Uncle Buddy had invited Barbara and me to visit them in Waldo.

Mother said that she could put us on the train in Birmingham and Uncle Buddy could meet us in Memphis and transfer us to the train going to Waldo. "What do you think?" she asked.

Barbara was very excited. "Ooooh, yes," she answered. "Frances and Anna are about my age, aren't they? We could have a lot of fun!" My interest perked up quickly. I knew we had relatives in Arkansas, but I didn't remember them very well. I liked the idea of taking a trip on the train. We had been in Jemison almost four years, but about the only place we had visited was Birmingham.

"You'd be safe, I think," Mother said. "We could make sure you get on the right train in Birmingham, and Uncle Buddy would meet your train in Memphis. Barbara is old enough to be responsible."

I didn't care much for the last remark. I figured I was old enough to be responsible without Barbara trying to boss me around. True, she was fourteen and I was ten, but I didn't like her telling me what to do. I started to make a smart remark, but I thought better of it because I didn't want to do anything which could mess up our chances for the trip.

Uncle Buddy and Aunt Lena had eight children—four boys and four girls, the youngest a baby boy, Butch. Wilma, Jeanette, and Gordon Jr. were about my age. Charles and Bill rounded out the eight. Having cousins to play with and a train trip to boot made us so excited we could hardly stand it.

We started pestering, but Mother and Dad wouldn't make a quick decision. They wanted to make absolutely sure we would be safe, so they decided to write to Uncle Buddy and have him explain again how he would meet us in Memphis.

It would cost some money, but fortunately, Andrew Price had improved our fortunes to the point that we could afford it. The big issue at this point was not money, but safety. Because of my previous accidents, my parents were very protective.

The more I thought about it, the more I wanted to go. When I went to bed at night, I would imagine what it was like to take a long ride on the train. After I went to sleep, I would dream about it.

In a couple of weeks, Uncle Buddy's reply arrived, and he assured my folks that nothing could go wrong. After a little more discussion, Mother and Dad decided we could do it. Barbara and I were both overjoyed.

UNCLE BUDDY, WHOSE REAL name was Gordon Summitt, worked for the Cotton Belt railroad. He had started as a section hand in 1918 and had worked up to being in charge of track maintenance for a three hundred-mile section of the line. The Cotton Belt connected St. Louis and Dallas. Along the way, it ran through Memphis and Waldo, the little town where Uncle Buddy and his family lived. The plan was for us to ride the Frisco from Birmingham to Memphis and then change to the Cotton Belt. The two lines used different stations, which complicated things a little. But there was nothing to worry about because Uncle Buddy would arrive on the Cotton Belt three hours before our train was due in from Birmingham.

It was decided we would go in the middle of June and stay in Waldo two weeks. I was so excited by the prospects that I wished there was some way I could make the time pass faster. This, of course, made the time drag even more. I thought the day would never arrive.

The big day did arrive. Mother and Dad packed our bags and took us to Birmingham. They gave each of us some money to pay for things when we were in Waldo. I had my money safely tucked away in my new billfold in my back pocket. We arrived at Terminal Station. It was bigger than anything I had ever seen, and I was in wonder.

A big board announced arrivals and departures and determined the track our train would be on. We went down a tunnel to a stairway which had the track number on it. We stood on the platform a few minutes, and the train puffed in. Mother and Dad put us on the correct car and stood outside watching until the train pulled away. My happiness was complete.

The train puffed along at what I thought was a fantastic speed. We went whizzing through small towns and stopped occasionally at larger ones. We had been strictly admonished not to get off before we got to Memphis, no matter how long the conductor said the train would wait at the stops. Barbara and I were insecure enough that we firmly obeyed our parents' warning. In fact, we never left the car in which we were riding.

After a while, I got bold enough to walk up and down the aisle. The train swayed from side to side as it rushed along. It was fun to run back and forth and try to stand up straight. Barbara didn't like for me to do it, so she told me to stop. This irritated me mightily. At first I didn't pay any attention to her, but she finally spoke in a loud and firm voice. I sat down, but I didn't like her thinking she was boss.

Finally I figured I could outmaneuver her by saying that I had to go to the bathroom. I went to the bathroom about every fifteen minutes during the six-hour trip. Barbara saw what was happening, but all she could do was stew. She remembered my third grade incident with Miss Mims, and she didn't want a repeat. Among other things, our bags were checked through, and I didn't have any more clothes to wear.

Finally the train pulled into the station in Memphis. We looked out the window, but we didn't see anybody standing there who looked like Uncle Buddy. Nobody came on the car and spoke to us. No adults looked as if they were searching for anyone. This was unsettling. We both had memorized pictures of Uncle Buddy, and we had been assured over and over that nothing could go wrong.

We stepped off the train and went into the station. We sat and sat. Uncle Buddy never showed up. This time I did what Barbara told me without any argument. I was afraid we were lost forever. Barbara knew the departure time for the Cotton Belt train, and she also knew that we had to change train stations.

Finally she said, "Something is really wrong. It's only forty minutes until the train leaves for Waldo. We're going to miss our train." She noticed that there was a desk at the side of the waiting room with a sign, "Travelers Aide." She said, "Come on, we're going over there."

She explained our dilemma to the people at the Travelers Aide desk, and they went into action. They got a taxi and took us to the other station where they checked everything, and put us on the right train. The representative told the conductor to watch out for us and make sure we got off at Waldo. Barbara offered to pay for the taxi, but they said, "No, it's our job to help you. You did the right thing."

After we had been sitting in the Cotton Belt car a few minutes, Barbara said to me, "Don't you ever tell anybody that we had to go to Travelers Aide."

The train left Memphis about 5:30 p.m. It seemed to me it was nicer than the one from Birmingham, and I was proud this was the railroad my uncle worked for. Before we had gone far, my confidence and desire to aggravate Barbara returned. I resumed my regular trips to the bathroom. I finally tired of this, and by 10 p.m. I was getting sleepy. I curled up in my seat and dozed off.

Before long Barbara shook me awake and told me we were about to arrive in Waldo. The train slowed and stopped. The conductor made sure we stepped off safely. Even though it was 2 a.m., all of our cousins, except the baby, were there to meet us. They didn't have far to walk because their house was right by the railroad track. They were surprised we were alone; Uncle Buddy and Aunt Lena had gone to Memphis to meet us.

We all went across the tracks to their house. It wasn't long before the telephone rang. It was Uncle Buddy and Aunt Lena calling from Memphis. Their train was late getting to Memphis, and we were not in the Frisco station where we were supposed to meet them. They were worried sick because they couldn't find us.

After the call, they caught the first train back to Waldo. They had gone to Memphis for nothing and had a big scare. When they arrived back home, Uncle Buddy was upset. He told Barbara, "Don't you ever do that again. If I'm supposed to meet you, I'll meet you. You sit there and wait."

Since I was younger and more innocent (and more petted, Barbara claimed), he didn't say anything to me.

A few minutes later Barbara and I were alone. She was all puffed up because Uncle Buddy had fussed at her. "I'll do the same thing again because I'm scared to sit there alone," she said to me. "He ought to make sure he is in Memphis on time. But whatever we do, you remember not to tell anybody about Travelers Aide."

We really had a good time in Waldo visiting our cousins. The house had a very large yard, with plenty of room to play softball and other games. I slept in the front room of the house, and I could see through a window across the railroad tracks to the main street of Waldo. There was a movie theater, with a whole bunch of neon on the front. I thought it was real pretty, and I was very envious since we didn't have a movie theater in Jemison.

It turned out my cousin Jeanette was the same age as me, and we became big pals. Frances and Anna were the oldest and were closer to Barbara's age. Being around such a large group was new for Barbara and me, especially since we didn't have any relatives in Alabama. The five younger cousins, except the baby, ran around their big yard all the time, playing and yelling. Francis and Anna had achieved later teenage status, and they tried to be more dignified.

Barbara was fourteen and maturing nicely. She had already discovered that boys and girls were attracted to each other. Frances and Anna introduced her to some local males, and the three of them had a wonderful time with the fellows riding horses, walking around town, and drinking cherry Cokes at the drug store. Aunt Lena kept a close eye on them and made certain nothing happened that a good Southern Baptist wouldn't approve.

The two weeks seemed to pass before we knew it. We really had fun, so we didn't want to leave. But alas, the day came. To prevent any unforeseen problems, Uncle Bateman and Aunt Olean Summitt rode the train with us to Memphis and transferred us to the train for Birmingham.

We still had some of the money Mother had given us for the trip. It got supper time, and Barbara said, "Let's go to the dining car and eat."

This was a great idea, so I went along happily. I had a hamburger steak and pie and chocolate milk and enjoyed it greatly. Barbara ate a small salad.

The waiter brought the bill, and Barbara said, "Pay him for yours."

"I can't," I said.

She gave me a dirty look. "Why can't you?"

"Because I put my billfold in the suitcase, and you checked it through to Birmingham."

Barbara turned red and was absolutely livid. "Here I worried and planned," she said. "I took care of my money so that I would have plenty to cover meals and wouldn't run out. Now you're making me spend my money for you. I'm mad as fire."

I could see she was mad. I felt guilty, but there was nothing I could do about it. "I'm sorry," I said meekly. She kept on about all that I ordered and how careful she had been with her money. She told me I seemed never to worry about anything.

I thought to myself, "Maybe it's best not to worry. When we get home, I'll have my money and she won't."

NOT LONG AFTER WE got back from Arkansas, Barbara invited her girlfriends to the cafe. She told them all about the trip and what fun she had with Frances and Anna. She went into great detail about all of the boys she met and all of the things they did.

Barbara's girl friends were smiling great big and giggling. They were really enjoying the stories she was telling. I thought it was all very silly, but I acted the spy and listened carefully in the next booth in case she said something I could use later when she and I were feuding.

FALL SOON ARRIVED, AND we were back in school again. Miss Brown, my new teacher, was not only pretty but was very sweet and gentle. Everyone liked her. I had plenty of ammunition that year when we talked in class about summer or about family or trips. Everyone heard about Waldo over and over. Miss Brown always honored my requests to be excused. I guess Miss Mims had passed the word to her.

It was a pretty typical school year for me. For the most part, the same kids had been in my class since I started to school in Jemison. We all knew each other well and had our special friends. Boys and girls were feeling the first stirrings, and they started pairing off as sweethearts. This condition required exchanging secret notes during class, out of view of the teacher. It was a terrible defeat to have Miss Brown intercept a note and read it aloud. Ability to fold notes in a very tight, compact square was much admired. The pairings lasted anywhere from a couple of days to a week or two.

Most of the boys had fights from time to time. These were generally harmless, with a bloody nose the worst consequence. The participants would have at it and then be best friends again in a few minutes. I didn't like the idea of a fight and carefully avoided them. As a result, the other kids started thinking of me as something of a sissy.

In the middle of the year, a new boy started in our class. His name was Kenneth Ray. He was a little bigger than the rest of us, and he quickly established himself as the best fighter in the group. He could even whip boys in the fifth and sixth grades. Kenneth was popular for this, as well as for his inclination to create disturbances during class. Kenneth and I soon became special friends. It was sort of a pairing of opposites—the class sissy and the class tough guy. The other boys, practicing the better part of valor, started showing more respect for me; a wrong word could earn them a bloody nose.

As Valentine's Day approached, we elected a new class king and queen, Mack Smith and Mary Catherine McNeil. Mack and Mary Catherine were both very popular, and we had great hopes for the contest at the Valentine's Day party. But Junior and Gwendolyn won again by a landslide.

WE WENT TO BIRMINGHAM every six months or so, and one thing that fascinated me was the streetcars. They seemed so citified and so modern. When we were there, I pestered Mother to let me ride one. She didn't see the use of it, but once or twice she relented and we went for a short ride.

I was so impressed that I started pretending I was a streetcar conductor when I rode my bike from the cafe over to town. I developed regular routes. It was about a block and a half from the highway to the railroad track. The dirt road went down a slight incline to a little ditch, and it went up again to the tracks. On one side was a dirt sidewalk which was higher than the road most of the way. One of my routes went down the middle of the road. Another went on the sidewalk.

When I got to the railroad, I could either cross there or turn left on a street which ran beside the tracks a block to the next crossing. Kenneth Ray lived on the street by the tracks, and his house was one of a number of regular stops the "Jemison streetcar" made. I was the conductor, and I announced the stops as I approached them.

I had great fun doing this, but for whatever reason, I never told anybody else about it—not even Junior or Kenneth. It was my own little game.

All of the kids had bicycles, and every chance they got, they peddled around. We would ride around town together. A favorite sport was to see who could peddle the fastest. I could hold my own in bike racing, so I wasn't a complete sissy. We were able to ride considerable distances. It was safe to ride to Thorsby and back or to go three or four miles out in the country without supervision.

ONE AFTERNOON IN THE cafe, Mother questioned me about Kenneth.

"He's a lot of fun," I answered, "and we talk and play together at school. Tommy Sharp was getting real mean with me the other day, and Kenneth told him to shut up or he would knock his head off."

Mother smiled. She liked the idea that I had a "savior," at least in the fighting world. She also thought it a good idea to give Kenneth glasses of milk when he came in the cafe to keep him healthy and strong so he could protect her son.

ABOUT THIS TIME BILL Dubose walked in. He sat down with Dad and started a discussion of WWII. Bill asked, "What do you think about what's happened to France?" Dad responded that it all seemed very bad and felt that the Germans could beat anyone. Seymour and Coach came in about the same time and heard Dad's last remark.

"Do you suppose they can beat England," Coach wondered.

"I think so," Seymour declared. "Nobody has come close to standing up to them. What does England have?"

"Well," said Bill, "England has the Channel, and nobody has managed to cross that in about a thousand years. If you read about the Norman invasion, it may not look far across there, but it's mighty difficult to force your way from one side to the other."

Dad also expressed his hope that the English Channel would do its job, otherwise all of Europe and the U.S. would be in big trouble. Dad knew that Hitler was a dictator, and we would have to deal with him sooner or later. He knew that the days of the ocean protecting us were gone.

I listened to all of this with a growing sense of fear. Bill, Dad, and Coach were smart. I wasn't sure what Hitler could do to us, but I figured it had to be something bad. Coach went on his way. Bill joined Edna and Seymour for supper.

Two of the young teachers came in, and, of course, they sat by Bill. Soon they were discussing the new song, "Fan It," and how suggestive the lyrics were. The young teachers thought the song was just terrible, so Bill got up, put his nickel in the juke box and punched the button for "Fan It."

The song was real country sounding. The singer had a good twang, and he pronounced his words like somebody from way back in the sticks. The song was about a girl he knew who got sort of warm in certain parts of her anatomy. Every verse ended with, "You got to fan it, Aunt Suzy. Fan it 'til the cows come home."

"See," said the teacher. "Isn't that awful?"

"I don't think I'll play it again," Bill assured her.

Just then, Bill Cobb and one of his buddies came in. They ordered cold drinks. As Mother was getting them, Bill Cobb walked over to the juke box, dropped in his money, and you guessed it, played "Fan It."

One of the teachers expressed her disgust and proudly announced one of her favorite songs was "Elmer's Tune."

Bill thought a minute. "Now let's see," he said. "Let's think of a line from 'Elmer's Tune.' 'Why does the gander meander in search of the goose?' You think that's worse than 'Fan It?' I think they're both talking about the same thing."

The teacher flushed. Everybody who was listening could see that, at a certain level, Bill Cobb was right. She finally said, "Well, I don't know about that, but there are right and wrong ways to do things."

Bill Dubose sort of grinned and tried to change the subject. I wasn't sure what they were talking about, but I sided with the teacher. Dad decided to end the argument and said, "Well, I think we all like 'San Antonio Rose.'"

They all agreed, and chatter continued as usual.

ONE DAY BARBARA WAS busy writing a letter. I wouldn't have paid much attention except I could see she was taking special pains and spending a lot of time on it. Also, she smiled from time to time, and the expression on her face changed with whatever she was putting on the paper.

Some of her girlfriends came along, and they all went out to sit on the wall in front of our house. Barbara had moved her letter behind the counter, but she left it on top of the stationery box. I knew it was none of my business, but I was curious to see what was taking so much concentration. I hesitated a few seconds before temptation got the best of me.

Mother was in the kitchen, so I was safe for a few moments. The letter was to Frances and Anna. Barbara started by telling them about the school year and about how we were getting along. But most of the letter was about Bill Cobb. She went on about how cute he was and how her heart fluttered when he made eyes at her. She said he walked around with his handkerchief hanging out of his back pocket, and that was just the most adorable thing she had ever seen. The handkerchief was one of those big red flowery ones like the workers wear on the railroad.

That was on the first page. She had finished two more pages and was going strong, so I was mighty curious about what was in the rest of it. But if I touched it, I increased greatly my chances of getting caught. Fear overcame curiosity, and I walked away. I could see that Barbara was stuck on Bill. I realized at once that I could increase my ability to irritate her by spying on them. I wanted to take a good look at the way he did his handkerchief. Maybe this was something I ought to try.

ONE DAY IN THE house, I happened to find a letter Mother was writing to one of her old friends in Arkansas. She was telling about our nice life. "We have fun every day," she wrote. "We have a picnic every now and then in the woods, a swim in Yellow Leaf Creek, or a wiener roast in the pasture with the neighbor children. Old Kit, our gray mule, and Babe, our beloved cow, stand nearby. They snort a little and seem to enjoy the intrusion of their private domain. It's a full and busy family life."

A few paragraphs later she wrote, "One of my most treasured gifts is from John. This year he gave me a five-cent Mother's Day card which included the verse, 'You enjoy everything you do.'"

I had just taken our life for granted, but her letter jolted me. I hadn't realized the card had meant so much to her, but it was true. She did seem to enjoy all the things she did.

7

Bill Dubose was sitting in the cafe one cold afternoon not long after New Year's Day, 1941. He started talking with Dad about the war and about how the British were still holding out in spite of all the bombing the Germans were doing.

"I don't think the Germans will be able to invade England after all," Dad said. "Those English are stubborn, and they're giving as good as they're getting."

Bill nodded. "I think you may be right. It's really surprising. Last summer after France fell, I thought England couldn't last a month. Churchill seems to have them believing they can actually win. I don't see how. But whatever happens, I'm sure we'll be in it sooner or later."

About that time Seymour and Edna Reynolds walked in. "Did y'all hear the latest news?" Edna asked. "We're going to get a new high school building. Mr. Peterson announced it today. Mr. Peterson definitely has the money, and some attorneys are authorized to advertise for bids."

That news made my eyes pop. I was in the fifth grade and would be in high school in two more years. Not really in high school in the usual way of thinking about it, but we called the seventh, eighth, and ninth grades "junior high," and the last three grades "senior high."

Mrs. Reynolds excitedly told us there would be room for both junior and senior high. "And it's going to be made of brick. It will be real modern with indoor toilets and a real laboratory for chemistry. Grades one and two will stay in the building where they are, but grades three through six will occupy all of the building we now use. They'll take out the classrooms in the basement of the old building and put in a lunchroom."

That was the big news around town for a while. The contracts were let, and the building begun. It was really something to watch. They built a concrete foundation, brought in cranes, put up steel framework, and started laying bricks. I observed all of this as closely as I could, but they ran us kids off most of the time.

BARBARA WAS IN THE ninth grade. Her special girl friends in town were Jimmy Ruth Dubose, Bill's little sister; Tommie Ellen Conway, the local dentist's daughter; and Dorothy Davis, daughter of the local taxi owner.

Barbara and Bill Cobb were pretty sweet on each other, and by the last half of the school year, Mother would let them go for a ride. It wasn't much of a ride. Mother insisted on knowing where they were going, what they were going to do, and when they would be back.

One afternoon Barbara came dragging in the cafe with a very sad look on her face. "What's the matter?" Mother asked.

"Bill and I had a fuss," Barbara answered. "And he asked Dorothy for a date."

Mother reminded Barbara that a new boy, Foye Guin, had moved to Jemison. Mother had heard Barbara thought he was really cute, so she suggested Barbara go out with him.

Barbara answered, "He has to ask me, first!" Barbara got her wish. Just before the end of school, Barbara came in one day very excited that Foye had asked her out. Mother gave her permission to go, with the admonition to remember the rules: first bring him by the cafe; and, make sure to be home on time.

The great night came for Barbara's big date. Two days later she was all upset again. It seems that Jimmie Ruth had selected Foye for herself, and she and all of the girls Barbara's age were mad that Barbara had gone out with him. Barbara got the cold shoulder the last few days of school.

Mary Thomas Cost, who was a senior and sort of the social leader of Jemison youth, didn't think this was right. She encouraged the seniors to take up for Barbara. This immediately raised Barbara's social status. Barbara was going into tenth grade, and normally, seniors had very little do with younger girls.

The seniors started inviting Barbara to all of their parties. Mother was not sure she liked Barbara being with the older group. She questioned Barbara as to who was in this new group.

"It's just Mary Thomas, Charles Littlejohn, Puny, and that group. Jimmie Martin and Leslie Glass are there some time, and you know they're nice. One I especially like is Doris Jean Smith."

Puny overheard this conversation. A little later, after Barbara had gone over to the house, he told Mother not to worry. He would make sure nothing happened to Barbara. By then Puny was a great friend, so Mother relaxed.

Doris Jean, her brother Mack, and their parents Fred and Norma Smith, had moved to Jemison the year before. Mrs. Smith's father owned and operated a planer mill, and Fred came to take over the mill. The Smiths lived with her parents, the Attaways.

Doris Jean was very cute and talented. She made good grades, and the teachers loved her. She was planning to go to nursing school at St. Vincent's Hospital in Birmingham and had taken the entrance test. According to Mrs. Smith, Doris Jean had made the highest grade that had ever been made on the test.

Mother felt better about it all. She knew the Smiths and knew that Doris Jean was a nice girl. She was happy that Barbara had a new friend.

I HAD A LITTLE romance that spring. I started making eyes with a nice-looking girl from Oak Grove. Her name was Marie Cobb, but everybody called her, "Scoochie."

Scoochie and I became sweethearts, and to show our devotion for each other, we met behind the lunchroom each afternoon after school and exchanged notes. The notes were full of the kind of things elementary school kids write to each other, like "I love you" twenty five times. We kept ourselves amused in class writing them and hiding them from the teacher. We would sneak to the back of the building, exchange notes, giggle, and go on our way.

I thought nobody saw us, but after a week or so, Bill Turnbloom started meeting me as I headed around the front corner of the building. Bill had plenty of experience fighting. He would torment me with taunts about my romance and about my fear of fighting. I was afraid of him, and I didn't know what to do. I didn't want to tell Kenneth or anybody because they would find out I was sweet on Scoochie.

Things were worse each day, and soon I was terrorized and in a real dilemma. I wasn't ready to break up with Scoochie. Fifth grade romances usually lasted at least three or four weeks. I certainly didn't want to tell her that I was afraid of Bill Turnbloom. He was getting bolder and saying meaner things and enjoying his bullying immensely.

One afternoon I gave Scoochie her note and walked around the corner, trembling in fear. Bill was waiting for me at his usual place. He started in, and suddenly, acting on pure instinct, I grabbed him by the neck with both hands. He tried to break loose, but my adrenalin was pumping, and I had a tight hold.

Soon he was gasping for breath and turning bright red in the face. He sank to his knees. I said, "You're going to stop doing this to me."

He couldn't get enough breath to respond, but he nodded.

I loosened just a little. "Are you going to leave me alone?" I demanded.

"Yes," he said.

"Do you promise never to do this again?"

"I promise; let me go; I can't breathe," he begged.

"I mean it." I said. "You have to promise and cross your heart, you'll never do it again."

"I promise. I promise."

I let go. He got up, dusted himself off, and ran off across the ball field. I was in shock. I couldn't believe what had happened. I had not planned it, and even if I had thought of it, I would never have had the nerve to try. I walked home, wondering what would happen next.

I gave Scoochie her note the next day, and Bill Turnbloom was nowhere to be seen. He didn't show up again during the three remaining weeks that Scoochie and I were sweethearts. He never said another word to me, and I felt deep satisfaction at getting the best of him.

ONE SUNDAY MORNING RIGHT after school ended, I went in the cafe for breakfast. Bill Dubose was there, along with the policeman and several other men from around town. Mother and Dad were talking with them, and I could tell from the looks of everyone that the conversation was very serious.

As I sat down in the back booth, Mother said, "John, something terrible has happened. Isn't the little Sunberg boy in your class?"

"Yes, Caroll," I answered.

"Some members of his family were in a terrible wreck last night between here and Calera. They were hit head-on by another car. Several people were killed." I was beginning to feel a chill.

"I think his little niece was one of the ones killed," Bill said. "And there were three or four more, including two adults."

Mother fed me my breakfast. The men kept talking, and I tried to listen. They didn't seem to know any more details. Mother kept hurrying me because I was about to be late for Sunday School. Barbara had finished her breakfast and gone to the house to get ready for church.

Everyone at church was in great shock that day. Caroll's niece, Irene Evans, and her father had been killed. Irene's mother, Caroll's sister, was in critical condition in Hillman Hospital in Birmingham. Irene's sister, Norma Jean, was also in the hospital. It was something we just couldn't imagine.

We learned that Mildred Sunberg, another of Caroll's sisters, had been visiting in Birmingham, and they were taking her home Saturday evening. It was about 8:45, and they only had three miles to go. A friend, James Campbell of Birmingham, was also in the car. They were all tired, and the children were sleeping. They were coming up the long incline just before the Montevallo cutoff. The two men coming the other way were drunk. They came down the road really fast, veered over, and hit the Evans' car head on.

The next afternoon, Mother left Puny in charge of the cafe, and we went to Calera to see the wrecked cars. They were smashed beyond my comprehension. I got out with Mother and Dad to look. It was frightening. There was a strange odor, and I thought it must be the odor of death. It was weird to think that just two days ago, these people that I knew were killed right where we were looking. Barbara wouldn't get close to the cars.

Two days later, Mother got a call. The Sunbergs wanted to have Carroll's classmates serve as pallbearers for Irene, and they asked if I would serve. Mother told them she thought I would be honored.

When Mother finished the telephone conversation, I asked, "Are you sure I can do that? I've never done it before, and I'm not very big or strong. Are you sure we can carry a casket?"

She answered, "Don't worry about it. It's an honor to be asked, and we want to help our friends at this terrible time. The Lord will give you strength."

Her faith was bigger than mine, but I knew I had no choice.

The funeral for the victims was on the next Sunday afternoon at the New Salem Baptist Church close to Thorsby. Other pallbearers for Irene included Junior, Mack Smith, Joe Bratton, and two boys our ages from Birmingham.

The hearses pulled up in front of the church, and the six of us moved behind the one which contained the remains of Irene. The undertaker opened the door and pulled the coffin out a short distance. He had us take the handles as it rolled out. We had to carry it up the steps of the church, and we were all straining pretty good. The undertaker took the handle on the back of the coffin to help a little bit.

We made it to the top, and the coffins of Irene and her Dad were rolled to the front of the church. The service was the saddest event that most of us had ever seen. I knew boys were supposed to be brave, but I couldn't keep from crying. My friend, Carroll, and his mother and dad were all in such agony. I felt so bad, but there was nothing I could do.

After the service we took the coffin down the steps. We had to walk with it a considerable distance across the church yard to the grave. I thought we were not going to make it. The undertaker kept trying to help by lifting at the back of the coffin. He helped those in back, but in the process shifted the load a little to the front. Somehow we maintained our control and dignity and placed the coffin safely on the straps over the open grave. I don't know how we did it, but as Mother had predicted, somehow we had the strength.

Before the end of the week, Irene's mother also died, and so did the drunk passenger from the other car. In all, five people died as a result of the wreck. The next week's Clanton *Union Banner* printed a front-page editorial stating, "Drunk Drivers are our worst menace. Four adults and one child are dead as a result of this most gruesome tragedy."

Being pallbearers got to us. Junior and I played and tried to have fun, but we just couldn't forget about it.

The Sundberg wreck continued to be a topic in the cafe, too. Different people talked about how dangerous automobiles are and how whiskey can cause terrible things to happen. Some wondered, in a more philosophical vein, how fate chooses a particular family for such terrible things.

Seymour and Edna Reynolds were in the cafe one afternoon. Edna asked Mother if it were true that I had been involved in a wreck, other than being hit by a car.

Mother explained that the story was true.

"It happened when he was three years old and we were living in Brasfield. We were coming back from a trip to Little Rock and were in DeValls Bluff. It was dusk, and a car hit us head on, about like the Sundberg's accident. We were knocked around some, but John was thrown out of the car. He was really hurt bad.

The axel on the car was broken, and we didn't know what we were going to do. A church was by the road. I was sitting on the church steps with my head in my hands crying and praying. Out of the blue, on that lonely road, an ambulance arrived. It was from Chicago and was on its way to Hot Springs to pick up a patient. They put John in the ambulance and took him to Little Rock. I will always believe it was a miracle."

It was a Catholic hospital, and all of the nurses were nuns. Mother recalled that when I started getting better, the nuns gave me a lot of attention. One of the nuns asked what I was going to be when I grew up. I said, "A Baptist preacher!" The nun laughed great big. My great-grandmother had taught me to say that.

Hearing this story made me realize that life is uncertain, and any of us could go at any time.

AS THE SUMMER WORE on, we got more into our usual fun and games. Mostly it was the same group—me, Junior, Mack, Kenneth, Bruce, and sometimes Joe Bratton. We liked to go to the other side of town where a gin, a blacksmith shop, and a grist mill were close together.

Mr. Northcutt ran the blacksmith shop. He drove a horse and buggy three miles from Oak Grove every morning. He put the horse in a little pen at the back of his shop and went about his business.

Mr. Northcutt was always working with iron and steel, and we liked to watch him. He had a little open furnace that he fired up the first thing in the morning, and he kept it going all day. It had a blower on the side, and when he wanted the fire to get hotter, he would turn a crank on the blower.

Several times a day Mr. Northcutt would put shoes on a horse, and he was an expert at it. First he removed any old shoes and cleaned the horse's hoofs. Then he would take ready-made shoes from a little barrel and custom-fit one for each hoof. Each shoe would be heated red-hot in the furnace. He banged on the shoe with a hammer and changed its size and shape. He could get a shoe fitted in just two or three tries. The last step was to cool each shoe in a pan of water and nail it on the correct hoof. I was always amazed by his deftness, the hot metal, and Mr. Northcutt's ability to keep the horses calm as he worked with them. Mr. Northcutt acted like he was a gruff old man, but he always tolerated us boys and answered our questions.

Right across the street was a gin, and it began working late in August. We all loved to watch the gin work. The final stage in the ginning process was for the seedless cotton to pour into a packing device. It had a big rectangular block which pushed down with great pressure. The gin people didn't want us there because of the danger, and they kept chasing us away.

It was also a lot of fun to play and roughhouse in the cottonseed bin. This was a small house which had a metal pipe coming in at the top. As the seeds were removed from the cotton, a blower sent them through the pipe into the bin. The pile of seeds was soft and a great place to jump around.

Sometimes when the gin was running but there was no wagon or truck under the input pipe, we would stick our heads in it. The suction would make our hair stand straight up. The gin people didn't like us doing this either, but they had to laugh because it made us look so crazy.

By July Barbara was having great fun, too. Mostly she ran around with Doris Jean. They had plenty of boys wanting to take them for a ride. Barbara was happy because she would be in tenth grade and would get to be in the new high school building. Doris Jean looked forward with great anticipation to the start of her nurse's training.

Before long a couple of boys from Thorsby discovered them. One boy, Leonard Bosworth, had a Model-T Ford, and everybody loved to ride in it. He and one of his friends started coming to Jemison and taking the girls for a ride. This was such fun that there were usually six or seven kids in the car.

THE NEW SCHOOL YEAR started, and all of the high school kids were very excited about entering the new building. I had made it to sixth grade.

During that first week of school, Barbara and Doris Jean were sitting on the front porch talking. They were discussing the upcoming week-end plans. Barbara's boyfriend, Leonard Bosworth, was coming in his Model-T, and they were double-dating with Doris Jean and Jimmy Martin. The great evening arrived, and Barbara left with her group. Doris Jean's cousin, Raymond Hubbard, Jr., had arrived from Birmingham for a visit, so he tagged along. When Barbara came in later that night I was already in bed, but I could overhear her doing some serious talking with Mother and Dad. I got up and joined them.

Barbara was describing an accident they had. "We were out on the dirt road between Collins Chapel and Thorsby, and we were acting silly. The car was going real slow. Doris Jean and I got out on the running board. Raymond, Jr., warned us not to jump. He had heard that someone in Birmingham had jumped off a car and broken their back."

Apparently, the girls didn't pay any attention to Raymond, Jr. The car was going slow, and the girls felt nothing could happen. Doris Jean and Barbara jumped.

Barbara continued, "I jumped. I had to run to keep from falling, but I didn't have any trouble keeping my balance. I looked back, and Doris Jean was just lying in the road. She didn't move. In a minute, we all urged Doris Jean to get up, that her lying there was not funny. She wasn't pretending; she was knocked out."

Barbara and the boys took Doris Jean to Dr. Franklin in Thorsby. He couldn't see anything wrong, so they took her home. They thought she was all right because she was talking. The first thing Mother did the next morning was to check with Mr. and Mrs. Smith. They were not at home, but Mrs. Attaway told Mother the bad news: Doris Jean had started turning blue at the temple during the night, and early Sunday morning was taken to St. Vincent's Hospital in Birmingham (the same hospital where Doris Jean was to have begun nursing training the next morning). The staff at St. Vincent's operated immediately.

Doris Jean seemed to get through the operation all right, but the Smiths were worried. We didn't go to Sunday School or church that day because of the worry.

It was hard to get any news with only one telephone in town. Two or three times during the day, someone got in touch with the Smiths. Doris Jean seemed to be holding her own, but her condition was very serious.

Darkness came, and we were all in a very apprehensive mood. Barbara was almost delirious, and Mother kept trying to calm her. I sat by myself in the swing on the front porch. I had this very strange feeling, like somehow the world was out of control. I was a helpless little nobody who could only sit and wait. I wished so much I could do something.

About 8:30 p.m. Mrs. Tom Glass came to see Mother to tell her Doris Jean had died.

Monday afternoon, the coffin was placed in the living room of the Smith's home. There were flowers all around, and the lid was open for viewing. It was the saddest occasion I had ever experienced, even worse than Irene's funeral back in June. The Smiths were absolutely distraught, and so was Barbara. In all of her grief, Mrs. Smith tried to comfort Barbara, and told her that Raymond, Jr., insisted it was nobody's fault. It was just a horrible accident. Barbara still felt there must have been something she could have done, and she had guilt on top of her sorrow.

The funeral was held on Tuesday afternoon at the Baptist Church, and it seemed everybody in town came. Brother Carroll delivered the message, and Doris Jean was buried in Pine Hill Cemetery just south of town. Doris Jean's death was really a shock to everybody in Jemison. It remained a topic of conversation for some time. The Smiths hurt deeply and continued to have trouble dealing with the loss.

One afternoon Coach Turner was in the cafe talking about Doris Jean when James Littlejohn came in. James was in the first year of medical school at the University of Alabama. Coach asked James, "What caused her to die, James? It didn't seem so serious when they took her to the hospital." James answered, "She had a concussion, and she also must have had a subdural hematoma. The trouble was blood collected inside her skull; if it's caught early enough, it can be evacuated, and the person will survive. But if it isn't, pressure increases and the person dies."

THAT THANKSGIVING MOTHER COOKED a special meal and closed the cafe early. The four of us gathered around the table, and Mother said a prayer of thanksgiving.

Barbara sobbed a little. "I don't have much to be thankful for."

Mother said, "I expect you do if you think about it. You had a terrible experience, but these are the things that test your faith. You must have strong faith."

"You need faith," Dad agreed, "but you also need the right outlook on life. Good and bad things happen to everybody. You can dwell on the bad, or you can think of the good. It's up to you. Think of all the good times you had with Doris Jean. For all you know, she might be a lot better off right now than you are."

"But surely I could have done something," Barbara moaned.

Dad responded, "No one will ever know the answer to that, and it doesn't do any good to fret about it. You did your best, and that's all any of us can do."

It had been a tragic year for Jemison.

8

Roy Acuff wailed from the juke box. "Listen to the jingle, the rumble and the roar, as she glides along the woodlands, through the hills and by the shore. Hear the mighty rush of the engine . . ." He was describing the "Wabash Cannonball," but he could just as well have been singing about the L&N. It ran right through the middle of Jemison and through the lives of all the people.

The L&N connected us to the outside world. People traveled to and from Jemison on the L&N, and its trains brought the mail. Everyone kept track of who got off and on the trains. In Jemison, everybody made a point of knowing everyone else's business.

One of the scheduled stops evoked special attention. Off of the train stepped a well-dressed young man, the nephew of the postmistress. The visitor was from Nashville where Roy Acuff and the country music stars worked.

One day, Charles Littlejohn and his cousin (the visitor) were walking down Main Street. I was standing out of sight behind a post watching a checker game.

"This is such a hick town," I overheard the cousin say. "I think I would be bored to death. Whatever do you do for social life?"

"Why would you say that?" Charles countered. "We have a great time." He described how everyone hung out at the cafe, a substitute for a movie theater, and how it was the gathering place after every basketball game and every other affair.

"Well, it sounds pretty blah to me," the cousin said with a final air. "What can you do with that old cafe lady watching? I think it's dull."

Charles and his cousin walked on. One of the men playing checkers said, "That city slicker needs some education. A five-cent investment in a Coke or a pint of milk won't buy you an hour or two of good companionship up there in Nashville."

The cousin irritated us, but he had a point. In Jemison, there wasn't much to do for entertainment. People listened to the radio, and on Saturday nights most folks turned to the Grand Ole Opry to hear Roy and his friends. Two or three times a year a traveling country or magic show came along. Once Roy Acuff and the Smokey Mountain Boys appeared in Calera, and we rushed up there early to be sure we could get a seat.

Such outside thrills didn't come often. Largely, we generated our own entertainment. Most of it was simply talking with other people.

As Charles said, the cafe had emerged as a major social center. The churches and the school added their part to the social scene, but they didn't quite complete the picture. The other key center of social activity was presided over by Charles Littlejohn's mother, the postmistress.

Everybody picked up their mail at least twice a day. When townspeople went into the post office, they were almost certain to see someone they knew. They would pass the time of day and exchange important information about people and things in town. Mrs. Littlejohn was in charge, and sometimes she or her assistant, Marian Glass, would say something, but not often. Mrs. Littlejohn had a strong dedication to duty.

The post office was about a block from the railroad track. It was in a nice building which had been a bank before the Depression. Along with many other banks in the country, the Peoples Bank of Jemison failed as times grew worse.

Several passenger trains came through Jemison each day. Most of them whizzed through, but two were locals and stopped. Number One went through about 8:30 a.m. heading north. It picked up passengers and delivered mail. If a person didn't own an automobile, riding Number One was the best way to get to Birmingham. The return trip was on Number Three, which left Birmingham a little after 4 p.m. and arrived in Jemison at 5:25.

People who rode one of the locals had to wear long sleeves and a hat pulled down over their eyes. The cars were not air-conditioned, and except for the cold winter months, the trains ran with their windows open. The engine produced a steady stream of cinders, a portion of which came through the windows. The cinders would still be hot, and they would burn arms and irritate eyes.

When one of the locals stopped, the depot agent wheeled a little hand cart to the train's mail car. He had sacks full of outgoing mail from the post office, and he exchanged them for sacks of incoming mail. Then he pushed the cart to the post office, where Mrs. Littlejohn and her assistant put the mail in the right boxes.

Small amounts of mail would be exchanged with fast trains which didn't stop. The station agent attached a mail bag to a holder on a little tower by the track. As the train went by, someone in the mail car pushed out a hook which snagged the bag. A bag of incoming mail was kicked out onto the ground.

People gathered to watch the trains come in, and then they followed the mail cart to the post office. The crowd for Number One in the morning was generally small because most people were working. For Number Three in the afternoon, it was a different matter. Almost everyone had finished their day's toil, and they were ready to relax.

Meeting Number Three was a major social event. A big crowd always stood waiting. The railroad curved about a half-mile north of town, so people couldn't see the train until it was almost around the curve. The first sign it was getting close was the clanging of the warning bells at the crossings. In a few seconds, the engine poked its head around the curve, and the train came puffing down the track. The brakes screeched as the train approached the depot and came to a halt just at the right place. Smoke poured out of the top, and steam hissed from the boiler.

After a couple of minutes, all exchanges of mail and passengers were made. The engineer then tried to ease the train forward. This required a delicate touch. The metal wheels on metal rails were naturally prone to slip. Sand poured onto the tracks from a container on top of the engine, but sometimes this wasn't enough. The engineer would push the throttle just a little too far, and the wheels would suddenly lose their traction and go flying around and around. "Choo-ca-choo-ca-choo-ca-choo-ca-choo," the engine roared and went nowhere. Then the engineer tried again and eventually had it going. It was a grand sight. Smoke, steam, and cinders flew in all directions.

A long procession then followed the mail cart to the post office. This was the largest mail delivery of the day, and it took several minutes to distribute. Everybody talked while they were waiting. In the process, the citizens of Jemison found out everything that went on that day. It was an efficient mode of communications

I thought Mrs. Littlejohn had been in her job forever, like Franklin D. Roosevelt and Mr. Peterson. I was surprised to learn that she had started the job in 1937, just a couple of months before we arrived.

I questioned James about his mother's job. James was happy to oblige. He told me his mother had been a schoolteacher but took the postmistress job because it paid more. It was a job that a lot of people wanted. James said politics played a role in her getting the job. The New Deal was going strong, Democrats had priority in the selection process, and Mrs. Littlejohn was most certainly a Democrat.

"A lot of people tried when the job was first announced," James answered. "When it looked as though she would get it, one of her cousins, Bill Steen, did his best to do her in. He wrote a letter to the county Democratic leaders claiming Mother was a Republican. You know, Chilton County was Republican until 1932. My father, Elbert, was a staunch Republican and a Baptist, and Mother was a Democrat and a Methodist. They didn't see eye-to-eye on a lot of things. The fact that he was a Republican almost cost her the postmistress' job."

He continued, "Mother had to get her voting records out and have several people vouch for her. One of the leaders of the county Democrats contacted Congressman Pete Jarman and assured him that Steen was wrong. He told the congressman that Mrs. Littlejohn was as good a Democrat as anyone, and that she was a smart lady and deserving. A few days later, Mother got a letter from Congressman Jarman announcing that she had the job."

I LOVED TO GO over to the depot and watch the stationmaster work. The depot was a wooden building, with "White" and "Colored" waiting rooms, both painted light tan. The waiting rooms had benches, but I never saw anybody waiting for a train there. The depot had a big storage area on one end with a platform for unloading freight. The really interesting part of the depot was the office, which had a clock, an old roll-top desk, and paper-stuffed cubby holes all over the walls. The stationmaster sat at a table with a typewriter and a telephone. The telephone had earphones, which clamped on the user's head, and a mouthpiece on a swivel. The telephone was for sending and receiving telegrams, messages for trains, and other railroad business. It allowed the operator's hands to be free for typing.

A set of three large handles with clasps on the top stuck up from the floor just to the right of the table. The bottom of each handle was attached to a metal rod which went outside to a large metal post by the tracks. The rods were attached to other rods which ran up the post, and the whole contraption was used to set signals on top of the post from inside the depot. Lights on the signals let train engineers see how they were set at night.

When we first moved to Jemison, Mr. Duffie was stationmaster. He resigned after a couple of years, and Mr. Jeffries took over. Both men were friendly with me and happy to explain how everything worked. They liked the company. They managed the depot, and in addition to their other duties, they sold tickets and handled freight.

I thought messages for trains were the most interesting. If the train was going to stop, the message was typed on a regular sheet of paper. If the train was not going to stop, a special thin paper was used. The message was handwritten, with great care taken for legibility. The paper was folded longwise and tied in the middle of a long string.

The stationmaster had a long stick shaped like a "Y." He put one end of the string, which held the message, through a little slot on one leg of the "Y" and the other end of the string on the other leg. Then he set the signals. When he heard the train coming, he stood by the tracks and held the stick with the two legs of the "Y" pointing upward. As the train rushed through, the engineer would lean out the window and extend his arm. He snagged the string with the message tied in it and raced on down the track.

I watched this many times and marveled that it always worked. It took great nerve for the stationmaster, because he had to stand very close to the railroad and the onrushing train. He also had to hold the stick exactly right.

I asked Mr. Jeffries how he learned to do that. He told me his grandpappy taught him, and told him to hold his tongue just right and keep his feet apart. He said a person had to demonstrate the proper frame of mind and prove he could stand fearlessly in one spot with fifty thousand tons of iron rushing at him.

I asked what would happen if he fell into the train.

He answered, "Well, I wouldn't have to worry about it anymore, would I?"

THE L&N WAS A main route from the Midwest to the Gulf Coast, and it carried large numbers of passengers. One source of wonder and pride to us rural folk in Jemison was the express passenger trains which went flying by.

Number Two looked about like the locals. It ran somewhere north of Nashville to Mobile, and it stopped in the larger towns like Cullman and Decatur. It would even stop in Clanton if there was a passenger to get on or off. Occasionally someone from Jemison rode it and added to their status. It went south in mid-morning and north early in the evening.

The streamlines were more awesome. Their engines were built with more of their innards covered, and they were painted in colors other than basic black. When we moved to Jemison, the L&N already had the Pan American. It was dark blue with a little maroon trim. It wasn't always full, but it managed to survive the Depression. The Pan American ran between Cincinnati and New Orleans.

After times improved, the passenger load increased, and the L&N needed more capacity. In 1941 the South Wind was added. It had a streamlined engine with cars built to match, and it was something to behold. It went through about ninety miles an hour. Jemison could never afford a street sweeper, and after the South Wind started its run, Jemison didn't need one. True to its name, the train created a mighty breeze and swept everything within a few hundred feet. An interesting pastime was to stand by the railroad at a safe distance and watch the South Wind rush by. We could see and wave to the people sitting in the comfortable seats and in the dining car. They would sometimes return the favor, thankful no doubt that they were on the train.

Later the L&N added the most magnificent of all, the Hummingbird. The Hummingbird received a big build-up in the papers before it started its run. It had every modern convenience and traveled at unbelievable speeds. There was so much excitement that everybody in town gathered by the tracks the first time it came through. We all wanted a close look at this marvel. We heard the whistle and looked north in great anticipation. The engine came around the curve, and before we could blink, the tail end was disappearing to the south. We learned that you could only see the Hummingbird well if you were a certain distance to the side. It joined the South Wind in keeping Jemison swept clean.

The L&N was very romantic and added to the richness of our lives. I liked all of the trains, but the one closest to my heart was the Hummingbird. It helped me through some of my chores. Dad, being a smart man, easily outwitted my schemes and regularly had me out plowing Kit. I didn't mind this too much. Kit did most of the work, and it was a better job by far than hoeing in the garden or cutting okra.

I could daydream most of the time. I just had to make sure Kit didn't practice the art of stepping on every plant. I knew when the Hummingbird was due, and when I heard the whistle in the distance, I would make sure Kit and I were by the fence where I had a good view of the railroad. I would watch the train go whizzing by. I would imagine I was on it heading to some exotic place, and would continue to daydream as Kit and I went about our task. Riding the Hummingbird became one of my secret obsessions.

THE MAIN TRACK OF the L&N was flanked on each side in Jemison by a side track. The track on the side away from the depot was used to let trains pass each other. The side track next to the depot was used for freight. Sometimes, two or three cars would be on the side track.

The boys in town liked to play on the cars. The agent wasn't supposed to allow it, and he would chase us away now and then. Most of the time, he just ignored us. Junior, Bruce, Mack, Joe, Kenneth, and I made a regular habit of concocting elaborate cowboy and Indian games around the cars. It was similar to the scenes in western movies. We could crawl around under the cars, get in them, push the doors open and shut, and even climb up the ladder at one end and run across the top lengthwise if we were fast and avoided the eye of Mr. Jeffries.

Kenneth could play cowboys and Indians with the best of them. We all knew, however, that Kenneth had a couple of cousins who lived a mile or two out of town. Occasionally, they would get with Kenneth and lead him down the path of temptation. One of their biggest transgressions in the eyes of upright town folk was to drink bootleg whiskey and get very rowdy.

Mother would hear about Kenneth getting involved, and she would give him a lecture. "You need to stay away from those boys," she would say. "You're a nice person, and we don't want you getting in something you shouldn't."

Kenneth would smile sheepishly. "Yes, ma'am," he would say, and as soon as he could, he would usher me outside to throw balls or something.

One summer evening about dusk, I was about to walk back to the cafe from town. I had been looking at some of the gadgets in the hardware store. I glanced out the window and saw Kenneth and one of his cousins walking at an unsteady gait across the park. The cousin was carrying a bottle filled with a clear liquid. The two of them made it to an open railroad car, and managed to climb in.

I left the hardware store and walked up the street until I was north of the parked cars. Then I slipped down to the railroad and walked very quietly to the car the boys were in. Very carefully and quietly I slipped close to the door. I heard Kenneth singing loud and clear.

"Casey Jones, he pushed on the throttle. Casey Jones, he . . ." Pause. Heavy breathing. Then there was a big thud like someone falling down.

"Oh, hell. Give me another drink, George."

After a short silence, Kenneth's melodious tones rang out again. "Casey done his duty like a railroad man."

9

One Sunday afternoon in December, Junior and I were on the sawdust pile playing cars. We had built a mountain and a road coming down on one side with sharp hairpin curves. At the bottom, the road went over a river with a bridge we constructed of bark. We pushed our little cars around our creation and pretended we were driving in some exotic place.

We had been out there an hour or two when Dad called. We looked up, and he was standing on the front porch of the house. He said, "Johnny, you boys come on over here. I want you to hear something." We walked across the highway and went in the living room of the house. On the radio was H. V. Kaltenborn, one of the well-known radio commentators of the day, telling about the Japanese attack on Pearl Harbor.

As Kaltenborn reeled off what was known about the extent of the disaster, we sat there trying to understand what it meant. Nobody said a word for a while. I didn't know about Dad and Junior, but I was dumbfounded. Finally, I asked Dad what it all meant.

He answered, "It means our country is at war."

"Are they going to bomb us like they bombed those people in England?" I asked.

"Right now we're only at war with Japan," Dad said. "They won't bomb us in Alabama because it's too far. But they might bomb people on the West Coast like San Francisco, Los Angeles, and Seattle, Washington."

Junior queried, "Do you think Japan could do that? I thought they were just a little country that made toys out of scrap metal."

"That's what we all thought," Dad answered, "but they must be more than we realized."

Kaltenborn read off the latest bulletins, and the news just kept getting worse and worse. Our dread increased with everything he reported. Finally,

Junior said, "I think I'd better go home," and he walked out the front door.

As the news circulated around town, everybody went home to listen to the radio. The cafe became empty, so Mother closed early. She came to the house, and we all sat in the living room huddled around the radio.

Barbara expressed her fear and hoped that we could whip Japan in a couple of months. Dad was not so sure, "They've been fighting China for several years. I hope we have time to get ourselves together."

According to the radio announcers, it was a total disaster at Pearl Harbor in Hawaii. They caught us completely by surprise, and our whole Pacific fleet was destroyed. We didn't have anything to keep them from invading California. Before the night ended, we heard that Japanese troops had invaded the Philippines, Indo-China, and Indonesia. These names didn't mean anything to me, but they all added to the image of a Japanese monster that was building in my mind.

I went to bed in a state of fear and with mixed notions in my head. They're just little twerps, I thought, and surely we can smash them with ease. On the other hand, they destroyed our fleet and were running around all over the place; they might invade California any time.

The next morning, December 8, 1941, the whole school gathered in the lunchroom, and we heard President Roosevelt give his speech to Congress. It was an event of overpowering emotion. He described the attack and asked for a declaration of war. He talked about the American people in their righteous might. At the end of the speech, President Roosevelt said, "We shall gain the ultimate triumph, so help us God." I knew at that moment that we were going to win the war. I knew that we were the good guys. I knew that God was on our side, and I knew that Franklin Delano Roosevelt would lead us to victory.

Those "little twerps" turned out to be a lot tougher than we had imagined. They captured the Philippines and our impregnable fortress of Corregidor. They took Guam and Wake Island from our Marines. They took the British stronghold of Singapore from several thousand Englishmen. We just kept losing and losing, and I thought we would never get the upper hand.

It really wasn't so long. We were all thrilled the following April when we heard of Jimmy Doolittle's raid on Tokyo. Maybe it didn't do a lot of damage, but we showed those Japs what we could and what we were going to do to them. A few months later, there was a movie about it, *Thirty Seconds Over Tokyo*, which we loved.

It seems that Doolittle's raid bothered the Japanese as much as it thrilled us. They decided to extend their defense perimeter by taking Midway Island. In June they began their campaign with the largest fleet ever assembled. Our side pulled the same kind of surprise on them that they pulled on us at Pearl Harbor, and they lost their four biggest carriers. Finally, after the longest six months I'll ever experience, our boys gave them the kind of smash we all expected from the start.

LIKE EVERYONE ELSE, I was extremely patriotic. After reading the reports of one battle, I said to Bill Dubose, "Isn't it wonderful that we're killing those Japs by the thousands!" Bill agreed but admonished me to remember that "war is a terrible thing."

Mother said, "Bill's right. Killing is terrible, and you shouldn't gloat about it. I'll tell you one thing, though. I can't remember a time when the whole country seems to be so much together. Why couldn't we get together like this to solve our problems back in the Depression? People argue about politics, but when it comes to war, everyone seems to come together. We could do a lot of good if everybody would pull together."

I mused to myself, "Why do adults have to pick everything apart?" It seemed simple to me: we were good, Japan was evil; and, the more of them we could kill, the better!"

We all wanted to help, and the government told us that one way was to buy war bonds and stamps. At every opportunity, Bing Crosby and other famous people sang, "Any bonds today? Bonds for freedom, that's what I'm selling. Any bonds today?"

The cheapest bond cost $18.75. Those who didn't have that much could buy stamps in twenty-five-cent denominations, stick them in a little book, and build up to a bond. I started buying stamps with my quarters. By the end of 1942, I almost had the book filled up. Bonds and stamps were purchased at the post office.

Periodically there were war bond drives. Every town was assigned a quota, and it was a matter of honor to meet it. Everybody would buy all the bonds they could to support their town and help with the war.

One time Jemison decided it wanted to be the first incorporated place in the United States to meet its quota in a war bond drive. Mrs. Littlejohn worked with the leaders in town to get it all arranged beforehand. Enough people agreed to buy bonds to push Jemison over the quota. At midnight the morning the drive started, everybody was in the post office, and Mrs. Littlejohn wrote up the bonds as fast as she could. Then they phoned in from Tom Glass's filling station that the quota in Jemison had been met.

We all waited with great excitement. A few days later, the head of Jemison's bond drive committee received a nice letter congratulating Jemison for meeting its quota so fast. It mentioned almost in passing that a town up in Montana had been first. Mrs. Littlejohn and the rest smiled and said, "Well, we tried and did our best." But me, I was bitterly disappointed.

THE GOVERNMENT HAD STARTED the draft in 1940, and they seemed to get really serious about it in 1942. In 1940, the draftees were supposed to be in for a year. A popular country song went, "I'll be back in a year, little darling. Don't you worry, darling, don't you cry." Those first draftees didn't make it back in a year, and by 1942 we knew none of them would be back soon, if ever.

Many of the young men volunteered. We were proud of all of the men from Jemison who went off to the service, whether they were drafted or not. Because of the draft, several went who weren't so young and, probably, would have been better off at home. No one said anything. We were all trying to do our duty.

LIFE WENT AHEAD AS usual in spite of the war. Well, not quite as usual. Early on the government issued rationing books which covered such things as sugar, shoes, gasoline, and tires. Most people couldn't take much of an automobile trip.

Just before gasoline rationing started, Mother had Mr. Burdette fill the five hundred-gallon tank attached to the pump in front of the cafe, so we were in better shape than most.

Junior's cousin, Douglas Glass, had one approach to the problem. Douglas got a really bad infection in his ankle and was out of school a year because the doctors couldn't get it cured. After he began to improve, his ankle was very weak, and on the doctor's advice, his parents bought him an Austin car. It was tiny and the only one most of us had ever seen. We were curious and envious. Douglas was only thirteen, but he was given permission to drive the car. It would go one hundred miles on a gallon of gasoline.

MOST OF THE TOWN boys went to the Baptist Church. Nobody put any pressure on us. Maybe at the start, some of us were pushed a little in the way Mother pushed me, but by the time we approached teenage status, we went because we wanted to. In fact, the majority of folks from Jemison went to the Baptist Church.

From time to time, the church would have a revival. A guest preacher would come in for that week, and he was supposed to be super. Since the war made the summer of 1942 a little different from those before, we seemed to take the revival a little more seriously.

The regular preacher, sensing opportunity, started working on us. We didn't talk about it to each other, but we all had this growing feeling. During one of the calls to come forward, a whole row of boys, including me, Junior, Mack, and Bruce went up. The next Sunday, we went out to Mineral Springs and were baptized in one of the lakes Wahoo had built. Just like that, we were members of the church.

Junior and I discussed why we "went up" that night. We weren't sure, but we felt we had done the right thing. We just knew we were a little embarrassed to stand up in front of the congregation and have people shake our hands and hug us. Junior said he didn't mind it except for when Violet Raines grabbed him and just about smothered him between her big boobs. He felt like he was drowning and was relieved when she went on down the line.

As the days went by, we settled into our new status as members of the church. It may have put a cap on teenage mischief for a time, but I noticed it didn't seem to make much difference very long. We seemed to go to church on Sunday and then do what we wanted the other days.

I began to ponder this a little. If we were the "new" people we were supposed to be, why didn't we act like it? I noticed a lot of the adults in town seemed to act the same way. My faith in the church's power to reform took a sharp jolt one day when I overheard a story told by one of the deacons.

This particular individual did a great deal of traveling, and he had been in New Jersey the week before. A group of men were gathered around him, and he was laughing great big and telling his story.

"We stayed in a hotel right down town," he said, "and when we went in the bar, all of these whores were in there. If you bought them a drink they would talk to you. So I picked a good-looking one, and I started buying her drinks. Before the night was over, I had her up in my room, and buddy, she knew how to do everything. It was something else!"

All of his listeners laughed and begged him to go into fine detail, and he accommodated them. I was pretty dumb on sexual matters, but I knew what a whore was. I could hear everything he said, and I didn't find it very funny. I was shocked at what he said and even more that he said it right in front of me.

The next day, I told Junior about what I had heard. I asked. "How can he be a deacon and pray in church, act holy, and then when he's out of town and gets a chance, do that?"

"I guess some people are just puttin' on," Junior answered. "Did joining the church change you?"

"I'm not sure," I answered. "Sometimes I think it did, but then I'm not sure. Did it change you?"

"I felt sort of 'salvationed' afterward," Junior said. "I felt something different as a result of going down the aisle and getting baptized. But I expected to get something out of it. What I really wanted was to see my mother and daddy back together. I've been praying a lot for it. But so far, it hasn't happened. As far as I can tell, everything is just getting worse. I'm so disappointed. The preacher told us we will get what we pray for if we have enough faith."

When I arrived home, I picked up Mother's Bible thinking I would do some searching and figure out Mr. Buckley's and Junior's problems. The Bible fell open, and when I looked down I saw, "First cast the beam out of thine own eye."

Coach Turner's daughter Ann was really cute. She was a year younger than I. While I tried to make eyes at her every now and then, Junior easily beat my time with her.

One fine summer day I was out riding my bike, and I went down the street in front of the Turner's house. Ann was out on the porch, and I invited her to ride with me. She climbed on the crossbar. I started off feeling pretty proud of myself, and I decided I would go to the old highway where I could ride a little faster. This was a short section of paved road that didn't have many cars on it. I rode pretty fast, and I started weaving from side to side to try to scare Ann. I leaned too far, and Ann and I both sprawled on the highway. She got up brushing herself off and giving me a dirty look. I started to say something, but my mouth hurt so bad I couldn't manage it. When I felt, I discovered that I had broken my two upper front teeth. After some searching, I found them. I pushed the bike home and showed Mother what had happened.

Mother was distraught. Those same baby teeth had the nerve killed during the car wreck when I was three. They were dark, and Mother couldn't wait until they came out and my permanent teeth came in. The new ones were nice and pretty, just what she wanted, and then I pulled this dumb stunt and broke them off.

Mother immediately took me and the broken parts to Dr. Conway's office hoping he could stick them back on. He just laughed. He told us we might as well throw the teeth away. The only solution was to take the nerve out and wait until I was grown and put in a bridge. He said my mouth was still growing, and a bridge now wouldn't work.

I was in pain. Dr. Conway suggested we wait a couple of days to let the pain subside and then start on the nerve removal.

Mother and Dad talked long and hard about my plight and a solution. I sat in the corner hurting and feeling like a stupid idiot. Barbara empathized, "It sure is a tragedy." However, I thought I saw a little satisfaction in her facial expression, like I got what I deserved. The next morning, Mother walked over to town and told Dr. Conway that we would start the process the next week.

The next day Junior came to observe my new snaggle-toothed appearance, and he asked what we were going to do. I told him. Junior wasted no time in telling me that Dr. Conway had filled a couple of his teeth, used no anesthetic, and described the pain he had experienced as a result.

"The last time I was sitting there, he was drilling away, and I was in terrible pain. I looked over in the corner of his office, and there was an old manual drill. It had a wheel on it so you could pump it with your foot. I thought, at least I'm glad he used the electric drill instead of that one. I heard he uses the manual drill to remove nerves."

Junior shook me up pretty good. I went home and repeated his story to Mother. The next week when we got to Dr. Conway's, Mother asked him about my concerns, and if he used deadening.

"No," Dr. Conway answered. "That's dangerous. If I did, the person I'm working on can't feel anything, and I might drill right up into the jaw bone and do all kind of damage. It's much better if the patient feels it. Johnny's a big boy and he can take it, can't you, Johnny?"

I mumbled something and we headed home. Now I was really terrorized. We went through drilling sessions every day for a week as Dr. Conway went down and exposed the nerve. It hurt more than I was capable of describing.

Finally, Dr. Conway said, "We're there!" He took a pair of tweezers and grasped the nerve and jerked it out. The pain was absolutely excruciating, more than any twelve-year-old should be expected to bear. Just before I totally disintegrated, the pain stopped. The nerve wasn't there anymore. Dr. Conway filled the hollow space with the goop they used for fillings, and we were done.

That night after I went to bed, I was asking myself what I had done to deserve such treatment. Here I am, just a poor innocent little boy. Then a little light turned on in my brain. It was probably just what I deserved for the little stunt I pulled with Ann. I felt redeemed. I had sinned, and the penalty had been paid.

As THE SUMMER ENDED, we heard terrible news. Coach Turner was going to be the principal at Isabella High School. Our great hero, our beloved coach, was going over to one of our big rivals. When Coach finally made his appearance at the cafe, we bombarded him with questions and laments, especially about going over to the enemy's side. He shook his head and told us he could not turn down a promotion, a chance he didn't get every day. He assured us they were not moving, and he would still be a cafe regular.

Barbara went off with tears in her eyes. "He's a traitor," I was thinking. "We'll probably never beat Clanton again."

SCHOOL STARTED, AND SINCE I was in seventh grade, I went into the new building. Now I felt very superior to the little ones back in the old wooden buildings. My feeling of superiority collapsed quickly. It happened in English class when Mrs. Duffie made us diagram sentences. I was puzzled as to what she was talking about and why it mattered anyway. Unless I could figure out how to recognize an adverb and hang it correctly on the diagram, I would be stuck there forever.

My desperation continued for months as Mrs. Duffie steamed on, full speed ahead. I went into panic every time she started diagramming. I just didn't understand it, and my little structures were never the same as hers. I memorized everything I could and tried to smash it with a bulldozer. I guess I muddled through because they let me go on to the next grade at the end of the year.

THE WAR DOMINATED MUCH of our conversation at school and around town. At first, our attention and been almost completely on the Japs and the Pacific. In the fall, Americans landed in North Africa and started fighting Germans, so we began looking there too. North Africa started bad for our side, but soon General Patton was winning battles.

Movies related the great deeds of our soldiers, and the newspaper had maps and stories every day. Edward R. Murrow came in regularly on the radio. Following the war closely was an obsession, and when the boys were together, we tried to outdo each other with our knowledge of details.

When we had a party or gathered for some other social purpose, we sang the latest war songs. With gusto! We sang *Coming in on a Wing and a Prayer, The White Cliffs of Dover, Johnny Got a Zero*, and *Praise the Lord and Pass the Ammunition*. Spike Jones helped us express our loathing for Hitler with *Der Fuhrer's Face*.

My favorite remained *Remember Pearl Harbor*. It was a stirring march with words that made me tingle:

> Let's remember Pearl Harbor,
> As we go to meet the foe.
> Let's remember Pearl Harbor,
> As we did the Alamo.
> We will always remember,
> How they died for liberty.
> Let's remember Pearl Harbor,
> And go on to victory.

10

By 1943, we were all feeling better about the war. Our troops were doing better, and so were the English and the Russians. In January we heard that President Roosevelt had met Winston Churchill in Casablanca. The paper had a picture of the president, a big smile on his face, sitting in a jeep with General Patton and reviewing troops.

Long stories were written about the number of airplanes, ships, tanks, and materials our country needed. Posters in the Thorsby post office and bank urged women to get involved. Much was said in the paper, radio, and movies about "Rosie the Riveter." Mrs. Roosevelt kept writing in her column about the marvelous contribution women were making. This irritated the Republicans. They were very patriotic, of course, but the tiniest thought of Eleanor provoked them to a fierce rage.

One thing we children could do was gather scrap paper and metal. Every now and then there would be a newspaper drive, and we were excused from school to participate. I liked this. I could feel really patriotic and miss a day of school at the same time! I pulled a little red wagon from house to house and asked for old newspapers to be donated. Also, people turned in their tin cans and old pots and pans.

The town boys my age were all interested in the planes our pilots flew. One afternoon a large group was in the cafe. In addition to Junior and me were Mack, Bruce, Kenneth, Joe, Billy Ellison, and Reid Adams. We were arguing the merits of the different fighters.

The conversation drifted into model airplanes. Making a model of your favorite plane with balsa wood, tissue paper, and glue was very popular. Everyone bought a kit and tried it. Reid Adams soon emerged as the undisputed champion of model-airplane-building in Jemison. I tried one or two, but Reid's looked so much better than mine that I gave up.

IN LATE SPRING, MOTHER received a letter from her sister, Gladys Lester. Gladys' husband, Jimmy, was president of the Teamsters Union in the Kansas City area, which meant he had a large gasoline ration. He and Aunt Gladys had been saving their gas stamps to take a trip that summer. Barbara and I were invited to go along.

They planned to drive to Jemison and stay a few days. From Jemison, they were going to Florida, then to Waldo to see Uncle Buddy and his family. Mother and Dad immediately said it was all right. Barbara and I were very excited.

Aunt Gladys and Uncle Jimmy arrived in Jemison in the middle of June. Aunt Gladys and Mother talked about the trip, and they tried to make sure we would be properly prepared. I followed Uncle Jimmy around and didn't pay any attention to them, but Barbara listened carefully. The night before we left, she said to me, "I heard Mother and Aunt Gladys decide on the amount of money we would need to pay our expenses. Now we have to be careful and not spend more than this." Her words went right through without touching my brain, but Barbara was all set for some worrying.

We drove from Jemison to St. Augustine, Florida. I had never been anywhere like that before and really enjoyed it. Barbara enjoyed it, too, but responsibility pressed on her. Later she remembered, "I calculated every time we ate. It didn't take any time for the money Mother and Dad gave Aunt Gladys to be gone. After that, I would hardly order anything because I knew we didn't have any credit left. But John just went ahead and ordered everything he wanted. He was happy as a lark and having a great time, not worrying about a thing."

"And," she added. "They liked him better than me. It didn't pay off at all, my being so responsible and considerate."

After St. Augustine, we drove across Florida to the Gulf and went swimming. I ordered sausage one morning at breakfast. When it came, it looked like little wieners tied together. I had never seen anything like that before. Aunt Gladys assured me that it was okay to eat and that it really was sausage. I stuck it with my fork a few times, but I never put any in my mouth.

We drove through Mobile and along the Mississippi Gulf coast to New Orleans. Aunt Gladys was so excited about seeing New Orleans, and she had gotten Barbara and me excited, too. When we arrived in New Orleans, Aunt Gladys expected to explore, but Uncle Jimmy just drove straight through.

Aunt Gladys turned to Uncle Jimmy and said in a very irritated voice, "Well, we went through there like a bat out of hell."

Without a word, Uncle Jimmy braked, turned around, and took us back into town for some sight-seeing. I didn't know what Barbara thought, but I had never heard a woman talk like that before. My Southern Baptist sensitivity was startled, but I thought it was pretty funny.

We went on to Waldo. Just like three years prior, we had great fun. Uncle Buddy and his family were in better financial shape than they were in 1940 because he had received a nice promotion with the Cotton Belt. All of our cousins were fine. Frances had finished high school in 1942, but she was home from college for the summer. Anna would be a high school senior the following year and was a real beauty.

Barbara was now seventeen, and she and her two older cousins were much more interested in boys than they had been three years earlier. The local boys took quick note of the Summitt's visitor. A couple of them were a hit with Barbara because they owned horses.

One of the boys offered to let Barbara ride his horse. She got on, and the horse ran away. The other boy urged his horse on and rescued her, just like in the westerns. She claimed she wasn't scared. "I just couldn't control it," she explained. "I knew the horse was going home and would stop there. I wasn't scared and wasn't about to fall off."

Uncle Buddy wasn't impressed. He didn't want anything happening to her, so horses became off limits.

The next Sunday the boys came back to the Summitt house with their mounts. As Barbara told it, "I was just dying to get on that horse. The boy was on it, so I climbed up there, too. I looked over toward the house, and Uncle Buddy was standing on the porch looking at me. He didn't say anything, but I had overwhelming feelings of guilt for the rest of the trip."

JEANETTE WAS VIVACIOUS AND could sing like a mockingbird and play the piano well. She and I became real pals. We explored Waldo, and she showed me all the sights that a teenager would want to see. I really liked walking up and down Main Street, just across the railroad tracks from their house. I loved their movie theater with all of its neon lights and the soda fountain in the drug store. They had Jemison beat on these things, for sure.

Our cousins still lived right by the railroad. During the war, soldiers would write their address on little wads of paper and throw them off the trains. Frances picked up an address from Merrill Vance, a young officer from Indiana and started corresponding with him. He was stationed at Ft. Benning, Georgia, and asked if she could visit. Uncle Buddy and Aunt Lena wouldn't consider her going to Ft. Benning, but Frances thought of an alternative. Maybe she and Anna could go back to Jemison with us.

They came and really liked Jemison and the cafe. All the boys fell for Anna, and this just made the Jemison girls mad.

Merrill Vance came over from Ft. Benning for a weekend. He was a big talker, and he and Frances sat in the living room talking the whole visit. Anna and Barbara hid in the front bedroom and tried to listen.

Three months later, Frances and Merrill announced their engagement, and they soon were married. Barbara and Mother said they thought it happened awfully fast. They thought maybe Frances should have waited a little longer. I was happy about it. Merrill was a captain in the Army, and when he put on his uniform, I thought he looked super. I knew he would go overseas soon, and I figured maybe we had a future war hero right here in our midst.

THE WAR KEPT GOING better for our side. In April, American troops in North Africa met up with the British Eighth Army under General Montgomery. They had been two thousand miles apart just a few months earlier. In May, we read about the trip of Winston Churchill to Washington to discuss things with President Roosevelt. They smiled for the cameras and made us all feel good. Everybody was optimistic.

Late in July we heard the electrifying news that the Italian government had ousted their dictator, Benito Mussolini, from power. He, along with Hitler, Tojo, and Hirohito, were the hated symbols of the evil enemy. President Roosevelt told us on the radio that it was "the first crack in the Axis."

American and British troops invaded Sicily the first of September. A few days later they moved onto the Italian mainland. This was very thrilling to a thirteen-year-old because it meant that American soldiers were now fighting on European soil. The Italian government surrendered on September 3, and we rejoiced with the thought that our side would occupy Italy and move to the southern border of France. The Germans quickly dispelled this notion. They held their ground in Italy and quickly moved in more troops.

We were all surprised in August when we read that Eleanor Roosevelt was visiting troops in the South Pacific. She received enormous receptions in Australia and New Zealand and toured American hospitals all around. She even went to Guadalcanal where fierce fighting had recently finished.

At school I deliberately sought out Joe Bratton and said, "Don't you think it's wonderful that Mrs. Roosevelt is visiting the hospitals in the south Pacific?" (I knew the Brattons were Republicans.)

Joe answered, "That old bag ought to stay home and mind her business."

"But," I argued, "I read where Admiral Nimitz said she was building up morale."

"Admiral Nimitz is just kissing his boss's fanny," Joe responded. "Everybody knows she is wasting the taxpayer's money. That's all the Roosevelts can think about."

"You ought to salute when you hear your Commander-in-Chief's name," I goaded.

"Go to hell," Joe said and gave me a hard look. Joe could whip me with his left hand. Since Kenneth was nowhere near, I knew it was time to change the subject.

The government had turned a Civilian Conservation Corps site in Clanton into a prisoner-of-war camp. The POW's had a pretty good life. They worked some around the camp, but mostly they sat around drinking beer. Chilton County had voted itself dry since prohibition, and we all thought giving the prisoners of war beer was terrible. We would drive by and look at the Germans over the fence. I expected them to look like devils, but they were about like us.

Many foreign soldiers were around, especially British. One day I was in the living room practicing my cornet and happened to look out the window. Two Royal Air Force soldiers were standing beside the road hitch-hiking. I played *God Save the King* on my horn to see if they would snap to attention and salute. To my chagrin, they didn't pay any attention to me. "They're not at all patriotic," I thought. Then it occurred to me that maybe they didn't recognize the tune.

SEYMOUR AND EDNA, BILL Dubose, and Coach were in the cafe one afternoon discussing the war and other matters. Bill announced he had developed a new process for making chairs. Strips of wood were cut into a certain length, steamed under high pressure, bent over U-shaped forms and bolted. When dry, the form remained. These formed the arms of the chair and could be connected to the remainder of the chair parts.

Bill was one of my heroes, and I was sure that he was going to get rich some day with his inventing. This time he had his brother-in-law, Jack Peterson, working with him

The chairs were very attractive, and Bill's friends believed he had finally hit on a winner. He and Jack drove around selling chairs off of a truck, and he sent samples to Sears and Roebuck, Montgomery Ward, and other big stores. Sears wrote back and expressed an interest. We were all excited. Before Bill's orders could come rolling in, Uncle Sam threw a monkey wrench into Bill's plan; he had received a notice from the draft board.

Try as he might, Bill couldn't get deferred. He was thirty-seven, single, and tried to argue he had an important business going. The draft board was determined not to show any favorites. In a short time Bill found himself in the Navy, and his one great inventing endeavor died on the vine.

One Saturday just before school started, I was supposed to meet Junior in front of the cafe. We were going to see if we could figure how to get someone to take us to Montevallo the next afternoon to a movie. I waited and waited, and Junior didn't show. Just as I was really getting irritated, he walked up.

"Where have you been?" I demanded. "You were supposed to be here an hour ago."

"I was listening to *Lucia di Lammermoor*," he answered, "and it was so beautiful! You should listen. Donizetti is a wonderful composer. He writes such beautiful music. I wish it had gone on another hour."

I knew better than to get in a conversation about what he had been doing because he could make me feel like a total ignoramus, which I was when it came to opera. So I changed the subject.

"It's only 4:30," I said. "Let's go over to the cotton gin." It was too early in the year for much ginning, but there were some seeds in the seed shack. When we arrived, Russell Peterson had a load of cottonseed he was about to take to Montgomery. It was piled high on his truck. Junior asked him, "How about letting us ride along?"

Russell agreed, but I didn't think too much of the idea. I figured I ought to ask Mother, but Junior climbed on, and he already had me with the opera stuff. I figured he'd have the upper hand forever if I let him go alone, so I crawled on, too. The cottonseed was piled high, and we hung on for dear life on the trip to Montgomery. Someone saw the truck leave and told Mother about it. When we arrived back late in the afternoon, she "let us have it. " I dared not ask permission to go to the movies the next day.

A few days later Junior came in the cafe with a sad look on his face. "Mother got a job in the ship yards in Mobile," he said, "but she can't take me because there's not enough room for me where she's going to live." Junior's dad had already moved to Pensacola for the duration of the war.

"Where are you going to live?" Mother asked.

"Mother made arrangements for me to stay with Miss Nancy Wells," Junior answered.

After he left, Mother said to Dad, "Can you imagine that? They're leaving the poor boy here by himself. Surely one or the other of them could make room for him. Miss Nancy is an old woman and can't do much for him." Mother told me I would have to be really nice to Junior.

"Well, I'll try," I thought to myself, "but he has to return the favor." It did seem pretty awful, not having his dad or his mother around. On the other hand, Miss Nancy lived only a half-block away, so he would be close by.

ABOUT EIGHT ACRES OF the land behind our house was used for a garden and to grow corn, wheat, and hay to feed the cattle. Dad wanted me to work out there. It was good for me, no doubt, but I didn't like it. Dad sometimes had me hoe in the garden, and this I thoroughly detested.

Dad was not easily riled, so he would be gentle as he tried to get me up early to work. Since I wasn't anxious to go, I hung back in bed. One morning, he said, "Get up, we have to go plow." I went back to sleep. He woke me up the second time and said, "It's time to get up. We have to go work." Somehow I dozed off again, and when he came in the third time, he pulled his belt off. I hopped up as fast as I could, but he let me have two or three licks.

Sometimes we would plow, and I had to round up Kit. When she thought it might be a work day, she went to the back of the pasture, as far from the barn as possible. Kit didn't want to work either. She was smart knowing it was a work day, but she was dumb because she always went to the same place. As I approached, she would look at me with big sad eyes.

Kit was pretty high strung, with a lot of spirit. Sometimes, when we first took her to the barn in the morning, she would jump around. She didn't want anyone to put the collar and harness on her. My dad had a "mule attitude adjuster." It was a little stick about a foot long and an inch thick on each side. It had a hole on one end with a loop of rope stuck through and tied. He would pull Kit's upper lip through the loop and twist. She changed her attitude and her behavior instantaneously.

Kit could manage to step on every plant when plowing a row of corn no matter what I tried. I would get mad and pick up a clod of dirt or a corn stalk or something and hit her over the head. One time, she really made me mad. I had heard other boys cuss, and I let loose with this part of my vocabulary. I screamed every nasty word I knew at the top of my lungs and cussed the mule out good. I happened to look around, and there stood Dad just behind me. I was frozen in terror for a moment, but he just looked at me and said, "Irritated you, did she, son?" That's all he ever said about it.

WHEN SCHOOL STARTED IN the fall of 1943, I was in the eighth grade, and Barbara was a senior.

Barbara was musically talented in singing and playing the piano. Miss Maples, a new teacher who started at Jemison that fall, had many ideas about how functions at school could be improved. She decided to sponsor a group of chorus girls, and Barbara became a member. They met after school with Miss Maples and practiced songs and dance steps.

The group entertained between the acts of plays. They had costumes alike with little short skirts and matching panties. At first everybody liked it. But one song, "Practice Makes Perfect," made Mr. Peterson uneasy. A local busybody, Mrs. Tapscott, complained. It was a disgrace, she said, for those young girls to be up there kicking and showing their underwear. Mr. Peterson took the safe path and put an end to the Jemison High School chorus line. Barbara and her friends were crushed, and Miss Maples learned something about small-town pettiness.

THE WAR CONTINUED TO go super well for the Allies. The Russians were smashing the Germans with help from the fierce winter. American and British soldiers were only ninety miles from Rome by mid-October. Our troops were island-hopping with great success in the Pacific.

There was no longer a question of who was going to win, just when. Popular songs, such as "Oh, What a Beautiful Morning" reflected the new optimism. *Casablanca* finally came to the theater in Clanton, and we raved about it along with everybody else.

"It's all so wonderful," I thought. "We're stomping out the forces of evil, and we're headed into a perfect world."

11

ate one April afternoon, Seymour and Edna Reynolds came in the
cafe for their regular supper. I was sitting at the center table, reading *Tom Sawyer* and eating bread and butter from a stack on the
table. Such fare made me plump, but I liked it, and Mother couldn't resist
giving it to me.

Edna was so excited. She had been at the county teachers' meeting in
Clanton that afternoon and heard some interesting news. Clanton was going
to start a band during the summer and have it ready to play at the football
games in the fall. Seymour deducted that since Clanton was a bigger school
and had a football team, they needed a band. Edna chided Seymour, telling
him that bands had more purposes than playing at football games.

I listened with interest. Playing in a band sounded like fun, and for a
moment I pictured myself in a fancy uniform marching down the street.
I didn't know what the connection to football was. I knew nothing about
football. Jemison didn't have a team and wasn't going to have one if Mr.
Peterson could help it. He thought it was a dangerous game.

After football season started, we heard people talk about attending the
games in Clanton. They said that the band really added something to it.
We wanted to see, so Mother took Barbara and me to a game. I agreed with
Mr. Peterson; it looked awfully rough. But I liked the band. We had fun,
so Mother took us back from time to time.

When Mr. Burdette came to deliver gas, we talked to him about the new
band. He had a couple of kids in school in Clanton. He was really proud of
the band, and he told us that the most important position was lead trumpet.
Mr. Burdette said that the person with this position in Clanton had played
before and was really good. His name was David Lee Parrish.

As fate would have it, two boys from Clanton came in the cafe the next
Sunday afternoon. Barbara was there, and they struck up a conversation.

Before long, one of them introduced himself as David Lee Parrish. When I heard this, my ears picked up. Here was the great trumpet player from Chilton County High School!

Barbara was impressed, too, and David Lee began visiting the cafe regularly. I watched him with awe when we went to the games. He wanted to take Barbara out, but when Mother asked Mr. Burdette about it, he advised caution. This made Mother doubly cautious. Until he could prove himself trustworthy, David Lee's interaction with Barbara was restricted to visits in the cafe. Sensing I was a great admirer, he talked to me about playing the horn and laid it on pretty thick about how great he was. I swallowed it hook, line, and sinker.

THE BAND LEADER WAS John Franklin Burton. He signed his name J. Franklin Burton, and had it printed this way on programs. He had taken it on himself to get approval for the band. He met with the county Board of Education, and after they approved in general, he talked them into allowing him to charge each student a small yearly fee. He explained that he had special skills and needs, and could not make it on a regular teacher's salary. With this arrangement, Mr. Burton's income depended on the number of students he could attract.

The next spring, the county paper announced that the band was going to give its first annual concert. They listed the program, and I saw with great excitement that David Lee was going to play a trumpet solo. I begged Mother to go, and Barbara supported me strongly. The band played well, we thought, and David Lee showed off his skill. Barbara and I were thrilled. Perhaps the most impressive thing was the printed program. It had very fancy type and included pictures of all the band members. Mr. Burdette told us that Mr. Burton did it all himself, using the typesetting equipment and presses at the *Union Banner*.

Try as he might, Mr. Burton could never get more than about thirty students in the Clanton band. In the spring of 1943, after a year and a half, he acted on an idea he had undoubtedly hashed around in his head for some time. He met with Mr. Peterson and suggested that a band start at Jemison High. Mr. Burton would meet with Jemison students in the mornings and with the Clanton group in the afternoons. As in Clanton, each student would pay a yearly fee.

Mr. Peterson called a special meeting of faulty and townspeople. He thought a band was a good idea, but he needed support. Everybody was enthusiastic, so Mr. Burton was given approval to begin the first of April.

Mr. Burton usually stopped in the cafe on his trips to Jemison, and I told him I really wanted to be in the band. I told him I wanted to play the trumpet. He looked at my mouth and said, "Your lips are too thick. You'd do better on a saxophone."

I was dead set against any such thing. Mother tried to persuade me that Mr. Burton knew best, but I wouldn't have it. It was a trumpet or nothing. Finally Mr. Burton said if I was so determined, so be it, but he would recommend a cornet because he thought it took less wind. Soon I had a shiny new cornet.

A GOOD GROUP OF the town kids joined the band. In general, boys took brass instruments, and girls took reeds. Mack and Junior took trumpets. Bruce chose a trombone and Joe chose a baritone. Ann Turner, Annette Reynolds, and Alice Dorr Denson all got clarinets. Mary Julia Blewster, Joyce Guy, and Gwendolyn Price opted for saxophones. Mary Edna Reynolds wanted a saxophone but was talked into a bass clarinet. The gender distinction was broken when Dorothy Ann Denson opted for a trombone, and Barbara Jean Price took a mellophone. Llewellyn Price and Kenneth started on snare drums. Barbara was going to be a senior the next year, and when she saw the band members were mostly younger kids, she opted not to join.

Mr. Burton worked with us individually until we could get a few notes out. When we started playing as a group, we enthusiastically produced a sound only a mother could love. By the end of the school year, we could play things like *Mary Had a Little Lamb*, *Twinkle, Twinkle, Little Star*, a fractured version of *America*, and a very simple march, *Activity*. We asked when we could play *The Stars and Stripes Forever*, and Mr. Burton told us it would be another month or two. It all depended on how well we practiced.

We were eager to play well, so that summer we met regularly at the Denson's house. They had a big pecan tree in the front yard, and we would set up our stands under the tree and play everything we knew. I noticed that Sam Reynolds, who lived directly across the street, drove away to check his rental houses shortly after we would start. But in general, everyone smiled and encouraged us. Marvin Headley, who was going into the tenth grade, thought the band beneath him. Trying to act casual, he watched us from the Headley's living room window with mixed emotions. Pretty soon his folks bought him an accordion. Our sound actually improved a little over the summer, and for once, we all were eager for school to start.

I MADE AN INTERESTING discovery early in the summer. If I said I wanted to practice, Mother would pressure Dad to let me do that instead of hoe or plow. Before long, I was practicing an hour or two a day. I was also freed from work when I played with the kids up at the Denson's house, and I became a leading advocate of group practice. Dad knew what I was up to, of course, but he could hire Jack Sales to do the field work. I thought I was pulling a good one, but thinking back later, I realized that maybe I was the one manipulated rather than my parents. I improved rapidly, and by fall, I was easily the best of the cornet/trumpet players.

WHEN SCHOOL STARTED IN the fall of 1943, Mr. Burton had everybody play individually for him. Then he had the band play a few pieces he had selected. A couple of days later, he arranged us all in order, with different ones playing first, second, and third parts.

I was the first trumpet, or as they print on most band music, Solo Cornet. Mack was second, and Junior was third. I liked this turn of events, but Junior didn't. He had been listening to his classical records instead of practicing, but he still didn't like me being first and him third. So he announced that his lips weren't shaped right for the trumpet; they were perfect, rather, for a flute. He switched to the flute, and, being the only one, he had first chair. Mr. Burton liked this, too, because it gave us better instrumentation.

Other students joined the band. James Lester Pate started on trumpet even though he was in the sixth grade. Since he was a beginner, he took over the vacated third chair without bruising his or his mother's ego. Sara Beth Sessions and Frances Hubbard, two new ninth-graders from Collins

Chapel, joined. Sara Beth played trombone, and Frances played bass drum.

A cute little girl from the sixth grade started on clarinet and immediately caught my eye. Her name was Louise Brown. She had dark hair, dark eyes, and dimples. Louise had the most engaging grin, and every time I looked at her, my heart went pitter-patter. I sent smiling glances her way at every opportunity, and she returned them. I found out she lived halfway between Jemison and Thorsby. Soon I improved my exercise routine significantly with regular bicycle trips the mile-and-a-half distance to her house.

SEVERAL STUDENTS IN THE Jemison band had made remarkable progress, and Mr. Burton decided to use us to beef up the Clanton band. He had only twenty-five players there, and adding eight of us allowed him to place an "S" at the end of "CCH" at half time. David Lee Parrish had graduated the previous spring, but he was ably replaced by Leland West. My successes at Jemison swelled my head, and I thought maybe I would be head man. But I found myself playing a weak second to Leland. Clanton had a flute player, but Junior, who was now practicing diligently, took over first. Barbara soon had second thoughts because she saw how much fun we were having. About two weeks after school started, she decided she wanted to be in the band. Mother talked with Mr. Burton about it. He needed a tenor saxophone, which was supposed to be easy to learn. He told Mother if she would buy Barbara one, he would let her join the group that played in Clanton.

Mother bought the sax. Barbara practiced hard and made fast progress. Being six months behind, she wasn't quite as good as the rest of us. True to his word, Mr. Burton let Barbara play for the games in Clanton.

Later that season, Clanton was going to Wetumpka to play. Mr. Burton wanted a big band, but he was afraid Barbara might make a mistake, so he didn't include her. The rest of us practiced all that week with the Clanton band. Barbara's feelings were wounded, and Mother's fighting spirit was aroused because she thought Mr. Burton had gone back on his word. She got after him pretty good. Under intense pressure, he agreed at the last minute to let Barbara go. The only time she practiced the routine was the afternoon of the game.

At half time we were marching around the field, and as Barbara described it, she was blindly following the person in front of her. We went into a key formation. Mr. Burton said something to her, and she jumped. Only she jumped in the wrong direction and was way out of position in plain view of everyone.

After we were home that night, Barbara started crying. She just bawled and bawled, unable to control herself. Mother, aware she had made a mistake in pressuring Mr. Burton, tried to comfort her. Barbara was too humiliated to be comforted. Barbara cried. "It was the most embarrassing moment of my whole life. I made a total fool of myself, and everybody saw me. My life is ruined forever."

AT MR. BURTON SUGGESTION, a Band Mothers Club was formed to provide needed support and help increase community interest. Mother was elected president. She was naturally full of vim and vigor, and she did a good job.

Mother and Evie Pate were close friends, and Evie was her able assistant. At first, all of the mothers got along well and worked together. They put up posters around town telling about the band, and they raised money to buy a bass drum. They had "Jemison High School" painted in a circle around the edge of the drum head and "BAND" in big letters surrounded by little curlie-cues in the middle.

The Band Mothers decided buying uniforms would be a good project. When they told Mr. Burton, he tried to talk them out of it. By then he had decided to have the Jemison and Clanton students always play together, and Clanton already had enough uniforms for everyone. He suggested that they buy some unusual instruments, like an oboe and a French horn.

The folks in Jemison didn't like the idea of wearing Clanton's uniforms. Their colors were orange and blue, and ours were black and gold. We had pride, and we didn't want to put on orange and blue. The Band Mothers went ahead with their project in spite of Mr. Burton, and when they explained the situation to the town folks, money was easily raised for the twenty correctly colored uniforms. However, Mr. Burton insisted we wear Clanton uniforms when we played at football games.

As the fall went on, the Smiths became more unhappy that Mack was second chair to me. The fussing prompted Mr. Burton to conduct another try-out for the trumpet section. I still held first chair. Under the threat of garden work, I continued to practice up a storm, while Mack followed his first love and played basketball with the boys. I was pulling away from him steadily.

Mrs. Smith, her perceptions blinded by a mother's pride, was sure I had first chair because of Mother's influence on Mr. Burton and accused Mother of such. Mother wasn't one to take such accusations. Her own parenting instincts were aroused, and she said in a loud voice, "You're absolutely wrong about that. Johnny is first because he is the best." The fussing continued, and Mother ordered Mrs. Smith out of the cafe. Mrs. Smith did not want to leave.

With fire in her eyes, Mother started walking toward Mrs. Smith, declared her crazy, and said that if Mrs. Smith did not leave, she would throw her out. At the last minute, Mrs. Smith walked out the door, yelling back insulting remarks.

This happened right in front of Barbara and me, and Barbara was distraught. This was Doris Jean's mother, and she had always been a good friend with us. Barbara was in tears when Mrs. Smith left.

Mrs. Smith decided she would challenge for control of the Band Mothers Club. She found an ally in Maggie Price. A few months prior, Mother and Maggie had a little spat because Maggie and Wahoo decided they would open a cafe next to his office across the street. Their cafe failed, but hard feelings still remained.

So the Band Mothers Club divided into two camps. When an issue arose, Mother's faction usually won. Everybody in Jemison knew about it, of course, and found it amusing. This group was supposed to be helping the band, but what they did mostly was fuss with each other about whose young 'un was best.

Mr. Burton was a rather hard-looking man whose manner suggested an arduous past. He stopped in the cafe regularly for coffee and occasionally ate a piece of Mother's super-good lemon meringue pie, but generally he was tight with his pennies. He got along well with Mother and took her side in most of the Band Mothers disputes. He couldn't afford to risk offending the parent of his lead cornet player.

He was a stern task-master at practice, and he used his sharp tongue regularly. Llewellyn Price was something of a prankster who stirred up mischief at the back of the band. Mr. Burton was irritated at him one day, and said, "Be quiet, Llewellyn, and pay attention."

Llewellyn sassed, "Well, I don't know why. I won't learn anything by paying attention."

Mr. Burton turned red in the face. He walked to the back and stood right in front of Llewellyn, and he said in a loud voice, "You show respect, young man, or you're going to find yourself punished severely."

Llewellyn started hitting Mr. Burton on the head with his drum sticks. Llewellyn's brother, Bruce, had to hop up from the trombone section to restrain him. The matter went straight to Mr. Peterson, who naturally ruled for Mr. Burton. Maggie Price and Llewellyn were called to a meeting in the office, and Llewellyn was read the riot act. At the next band practice, Llewellyn apologized to Mr. Burton in front of all of us. Maggie stood in the back of the room to make sure he didn't falter.

Kenneth Ray took great offense at this. He wasn't much of a scholar anyway and was disposed to challenge authority. He thought Llewellyn shouldn't have apologized, and he said so aloud to another of the band members. Mr. Burton whirled around and said in a very stern voice, "The proper respect is going to be shown by Llewellyn and by you and by everyone else who plays in the band. Do you understand that?"

Kenneth turned red and stared straight at the little band director. We all held our breath because we knew Kenneth could tie Mr. Burton in two knots without even working up a sweat. After pondering a minute, Kenneth put his drum sticks down and walked out. He never played in the band again

Once, when we were practicing for a concert, Mr. Burton was unhappy with our performance. He had finally let us play *The Stars and Stripes Forever*, and we sounded like the beginners we were. We didn't do well with the other numbers. He wanted us to sit straight and do better. As he was talking, I started making gooey eyes at Louise Brown. He saw I wasn't paying attention and whacked me hard across the leg with his baton. It hurt, and

I had a red whelp on my leg for several days. I didn't tell Mother about it.

AFTER THE BAND HAD been going a couple of years, rumors began to float around Jemison that Mr. Burton was carrying on with one of the local ladies. Neither Edna nor Mother believed the rumors.

A few days later, I happened to be exploring behind a big sign next to the highway on the edge of our property. A car, which looked just like Mr. Burton's, drove up the old highway and stopped behind the filling station. A door opened, and out from the bushes slipped the lady in question. She got in the car and held her head down so nobody could see her. The car drove off to the south. I didn't tell anybody what I saw. I figured this might be good information to hold in reserve.

THE FIRST ANNUAL CONCERT of the Jemison High School Band was held the spring of 1944, after we had been in operation a little more than a year. Thirty-five musicians were on the stage, thirteen from Jemison and twenty-two from Clanton. By then it was firmly fixed that "the band" included the players from both schools. I played a solo, *Little Home on the Farm*, and since this performance was in Jemison, I was first chair.

In the middle of the concert we played *American Patrol*. Our arrangement included brief excerpts from a number of patriotic songs, including *Dixie*. When we went into *Dixie*, Fanny Langston stood up, gave a rebel yell, and stood swaying from side to side. Everybody else stood up, too.

Mother was very proud of me and the fact that I had played a solo. A few days later she embarrassed me mightily in front of the cafe regulars. "When he stood up to play his solo, he really meant business," Mother bragged. "He pushed his sleeves back, set his feet, took his horn in his hands, and looked very determined. You know, I think John plays just like Harry James. He holds the horn the same way, and he even sounds the same!"

I was mortified. Edna grimaced, and Coach let a chuckle slip out. One of the teachers changed the subject.

TOWARD THE END OF the 1943–44 school year, Mr. Burton gave everyone copies of an announcement that a band camp was to be held that summer at the University of Alabama. Barbara was finishing high school and had decided to go to Auburn University, but she wanted to go to the camp. She encouraged me, and soon, with prodding, Mother and Dad agreed.

The camp band had twenty in the cornet/trumpet section. I was placed in the fifth chair, and, sadly, Mack was at the very end, fifteen places down from me.

I had a wonderful time at band camp and really enjoyed running around the campus. The camp band director was Colonel Carlton K. Butler, who also directed the University band. We loved Colonel Butler, and every one talked enthusiastically about the Alabama Million Dollar Band. I was really impressed. They also talked a lot about the Crimson Tide, the University's football team. I had never paid much attention to college football, but I became a total convert that summer. Back home, I was a rabid Crimson Tide fan, and I had my life's ambition—to play in the Million Dollar Band. Crimson and white became my favorite colors, and I learned how to play *Yea Alabama* on my horn.

I couldn't figure Barbara out. She had a good time and made some new friends, but it didn't change her mind about going to Auburn.

WHEN SCHOOL STARTED THAT fall, I was a solid second to Leland West on the cornet. Leland was a senior, and I knew I was heir apparent. Ann Turner was about as good on clarinet as I was on cornet, and Annette was a close second. Mary Julia Blewster was very good on saxophone. Junior was the best flute player, Joe was the best baritone player, and Mary Edna was unchallenged on bass clarinet. The Jemison group was taking over all of the top positions. This irritated the Clanton residents and delighted us. We liked it so much that we all practiced hard to make sure we could complete the conquest. It turned out that they had twice as many players as we had, but we were twice as good.

12

B y 1944 the Jemison Cafe was a well-known institution. The war ended hard times, and everybody had some money. Jemison folks could eat out when they wanted, and business was good. Wahoo continued to draw more and more patients for his herb-doctoring. He still made a significant contribution to our well-being, but by the third year of the war, the cafe would have prospered without him.

Jemison was halfway between Birmingham and Montgomery, and people driving back and forth had discovered the delicious food. Yankees from the Midwest even stopped on their way to Florida. The war was going so well that people didn't feel bad any more about using more gas than their ration status allowed them.

Getting good help was a problem for most businesses during the war, but it didn't bother us. From the first day Mother opened the cafe, Jack Sales' daughters had been her helpers. Annie B. was first. She went her way three years later and was replaced by Lummie, who married a handsome soldier and went north. Jimmie was next in line.

We were secure about help because Katie was three years younger and clearly of a mind to continue the tradition. Jack sired another daughter while he was well into middle age, so we figured he and wife Vicie could keep up their contribution a few years more. Everything was going well.

Two of the customers from Birmingham were an older man and his wife. Every time the man started to pay, he would argue about the bill. Sales tax was 2.3 percent, and if the bill plus tax didn't come out even, Mother would round up to the next penny. A bill of $4.25 and one-fourth cent would be charged at $4.26. This particular customer would figure it out and argue that he should only pay $4.25. The man argued that if the tax was less than a half cent, it should be rounded down, and if it was a half cent or more, it should be rounded up.

One day they came in and had two plate lunches, which cost seventy-five cents each. He went to the cash register to pay, and Mother said, "One dollar and fifty-four cents."

Again, he started arguing. Mother's face flushed, and I could see her dander getting up. She explained that she had to pay all of the tax that was due. "I have a business to run, and I don't have time to do those calculations. It's less than a penny. Nobody cares about that. They'd rather have fast service."

"I care about it," the man answered, "and when I come in here, we're going to do it right."

Mother looked him straight in the eye and said in no uncertain terms, "You're wrong about that because you're not coming in here anymore. We don't want you, and don't come back." He and his wife left, and we never saw them again.

WE'D ACCEPTED COACH BEING at Isabella. He was the principal and basketball coach, and this gave the Jemison-Isabella games special interest. He continued to live in Jemison, and he came in the cafe as often as ever. We still loved him and only wished him misfortune the two times each year our teams played.

One afternoon after school, Coach came in for his usual Coke. The subject of war arose. He mentioned that our bombers were raiding Berlin. He surmised Hitler had not counted on this, but Hitler was getting what he asked for.

"With all this action, I've been wondering if y'all have heard anything about Bill Dubose?" Coach asked.

Edna answered, "I heard he'd completed all of his training and should go out on a ship soon."

"What about Lester Pate?"

"Lester is in San Diego," Mother said. "I think they've decided he's too old to be on a ship. It looks like he'll have a desk job at the naval base. Evie took James Lester out there, you know, and they're living in a little apartment. I get a letter from her every two or three weeks."

Edna chimed in, "Today I heard that Irvin Beasley's family got a telegram saying he had been killed in action."

"What a tragedy," Coach exclaimed. "He was one of the finest young men I have known. I think he had become a pilot and an officer. Do they know what happened?"

Edna answered, "Apparently he was flying a B-17 on a raid over Germany and was shot down."

Irvin Beasley was one of my heroes. These kinds of messages came to people around town pretty often. It was a terrible downside of the war even though our forces were doing well.

The newspapers kept speculating about when we would invade France. A large number of American soldiers were in England, and it was obvious that the Allies were going to try to cross the English Channel. The newspapers referred to the unknown date of the invasion as "D-Day."

Late one Friday afternoon, Seymour and Edna came in to have their evening meal, excited over the news that Rome fell. "What's even more wonderful is that the German general evacuated the city, and all of the monuments were preserved," Edna exclaimed.

I went to bed that night after we listened to H. V. Kaltenborn describe the welcome our troops received in Rome. It was obvious the Romans were really happy to see us. I felt wonderful, but Dad made a crack under his breath about how the same people used to cheer Mussolini.

I was sleeping soundly the next morning when Mother shook me gently and said, "John, wake up. It's D-Day."

It was a magic moment. I jumped out of bed and ran into the living room so I could listen to the radio. The Americans and British had landed successfully on Normandy and things seemed to be going well.

To me this was the most thrilling moment of the war. We had been talking and hearing about it so long. I listened all day, and that night as I got ready to go to bed, I took a red crayon and put a circle around the date, June 6, 1944.

A few days later we read in the paper that the Germans had used a secret weapon which Hitler said would turn the tide back to them. It was something fearful, called a "flying bomb," rockets of some kind or other which were shot from the coast of France or Belgium. Dad explained, "They don't need a pilot and are a lot cheaper than trying to send bombers."

"Are they really going to change the war?" Mother asked.

"Not a chance," Dad said. "The bombs are landing mostly on London, and since there's no way to guide them, they hit everything, including houses, schools, and hospitals. It shows the German mentality. It will just make the British madder and more determined. Hitler and his boneheads forget that they dropped thousands of tons of bombs on London in 1940, and it backfired on them."

WHILE WE FOLLOWED EVENTS in France that summer, Barbara prepared to go to college. Even though I was planning to cheer for the Crimson Tide and play in the Million Dollar Band, I found Barbara's preparations for Auburn exciting. The great day when she would start was drawing near, and Mother wanted us all to drive her to Auburn so we could see the campus and check out her dorm. It came as a great surprise that Barbara didn't want us to take her.

The problem was our car. Barbara and I were dreadfully ashamed of our 1933 Chevrolet. Big changes had occurred in automobile designs between 1933 and 1941, and ours looked like something from the 1920s. Barbara didn't want to go to Auburn in our ancient automobile, so she announced that she wanted to take the bus. This wounded Mother and Dad, but they finally agreed to it.

The great day arrived. At the appointed hour, we went to the bus station. The bus pulled up, and we helped Barbara load her belongings. She sat next to a window, and as the bus pulled away, she waved.

We walked to the house and went inside. Mother headed for the front bedroom, threw herself on the bed, and began to sob hysterically. Puzzled, I walked into the bedroom and asked, "Why are you crying? I thought this was what we've been working and planning for all these years."

Mother looked up and couldn't suppress a grin. She sobbed a little more, got up, and went back to work in the cafe. In a few days Barbara called and assured us that she was doing well. She had already made some friends, and they were teaching her to yell, "War Eagle."

Seymour Reynolds bought our car in 1944 for $500. It cost only $750 when it was new, eleven years before! The Reynolds, who hadn't had a car, rode around in the '33 with great pride.

WE WERE STILL MILKING our cows, and Dad managed regularly to have me participate. It only took a half-hour or so, and he said I could spare that much time from practicing. My favorite cow was Ole Babe. She was a peaceful soul who gave us every bit of milk she had. She loved people. She would follow me around in the pasture, hoping I would pet her. I never saw another cow do that. The others kept their distance and would run if I tried to approach them.

We had five milk cows, but we didn't have a bull. When a cow began feeling romantic, she had to find a boyfriend or she would stop giving milk. Mr. Norwood, who lived about two miles away, had a nice bull, and Dad made a deal for Mr. Norwood's bull to take care of the cow's need.

My job on these occasions was to put a rope around the cow's neck and lead her to Mr. Norwood's pasture. I watched all of the romantic activities, and a lot of my confusions about sex were cleared up. I think Dad let me do it because he knew he failed the time I thought he was talking about a box of dirt.

Mr. Norwood's pasture was large, with a few acres in the woods. Ordinarily, the bull was nowhere to be seen because he liked exploring in the trees. But when I came over with a cow, he would be right by the fence, prancing up and down and snorting. I thought, "This bull knows something I don't; if I could only ask him a few questions."

MY TRUE LOVE WAS Louise Brown. We sat together on band trips and sometimes went to parties together. I rode to her house on my bicycle almost every Sunday afternoon. The boys kidded me about what I was doing with Louise, and I tried to look suave and leave them guessing. The truth was I never once made any kind of pass. She seemed so sweet and innocent, I figured I had to protect her honor. Besides I was very timid about such things, and I was afraid Louise would ditch me if I tried something I shouldn't.

One night after a play at school, Louise came with her brother to the cafe. She and I sat in a booth together, and her brother Bobby sat on a stool. Paul Northcutt, who graduated from Jemison High in 1941, came walking in. To my irritation, he sat in the booth with Louise and me. Paul started flirting with Louise. Immediately, I went into a jealous rage. I glared at him with all my energy, but he didn't even notice me. Louise was a child in Paul's eyes. He was just kidding her and having a little fun. I realized it about a day later. For years I cringed every time I thought about it.

Two of my good friends were Kenneth and Joe. They weren't very much alike, but they shared the distinction of being the two best fighters in town.

Kenneth's father died when he was a baby, and his mother married Henry Watson, a laborer who never managed to make much money. Mother liked Kenneth, and she figured it was her duty to help him rise to greater heights. She tried to give Kenneth good advice, and she encouraged his friendship with me, partly because she knew I was helpless in a fight. Sometimes I would go home with him for supper. His mother really knew how to make good biscuits, and I would put big chunks of butter on her hot biscuits and eat to my heart's content.

I was not athletically inclined at all, and it worried Mother that I didn't get enough exercise. She would give Kenneth a hamburger and a pint of milk to throw a baseball back and forth with me in the back yard. Kenneth kept his devilish side under control most of the time. Every now and then temptation got the best of him, and he would zing one over. Once he threw so hard that I missed with my glove, and the ball hit me in the head. I wobbled and saw stars for a few moments.

Joe, on the other hand, came from a relatively prosperous family. His Dad owned a grocery and a dry-goods store in Jemison. Joe was a good student. His aim was to make money when he grew up. He figured the way to make sure he acquired it was to learn as much as he could. He was tough as nails. He figured he could whip anybody, and he regularly proved it with boys who were older and larger. Joe could whip anybody—except Kenneth.

Joe and I had been in the same class since second grade, and we had a lot in common. We were usually the two best male students in a class. Joe had me up to his bedroom one night, and he showed me how to dissect a frog. The poor creature was alive and kicking when Joe started, and I was glad I didn't have to touch it. Another time, Joe and I were doing a chemical experiment in the back room of the cafe. We poured in an ingredient, and it exploded. No one was hurt, but it made a big impression on Mother and the customers.

One time, Kenneth and I hatched up a scheme to get Joe. Our plan was to go to the lumber yard across the street and play a game. Joe would be the sheriff, and Kenneth would be a bank robber. Kenneth would get Joe chasing him and run by a particular lumber stack where I was hidden. Just as Joe ran by, I would lift up a board and trip him. It worked to perfection, except Joe hit the board a lot harder than we expected. Joe screamed and fell over, holding his legs. Kenneth and I were afraid he had broken something, but he recovered after a few minutes. Joe glared at me. Except for Kenneth, I would have been smashed to smithereens.

A FEW DAYS LATER, Billy Ellison walked in the cafe and announced he was joining the Navy. He thought maybe he would be sent to the Pacific. Mother told him he should finish high school and then join. Billy proudly countered that he had already signed the papers. We experienced pride and sadness at the same time.

ONE DAY, SEVERAL OF us were standing in front of Murray Glass's store. Charles Watley said, "Y'all all come on over to my house. I wanna show you something."

When we arrived, he pulled out a bottle of whiskey. His mother and dad were working, and we were in the house alone. Charles said, "Let's all have a drink."

Mack and Joe took a swig, and Mack said, "Here, Johnny, it's your turn." I told them I would pass. I knew I shouldn't do it.

"What's the matter?" Junior taunted. "What will a little sip hurt?"

"I just don't think I want any," I answered.

The taunts began. Though I didn't want to and knew I shouldn't, the pressure was greater than I could resist, so I took the bottle and swallowed a little. It was terrible, and I thought I was going to throw up. I held on, and after Junior took his drink, we went back to town.

A Saturday afternoon two weeks later, Mack came marching into the cafe, followed by Charles Watley and Tommy Sharp. Mack said to Mother, "I just thought you'd like to know, Mrs. Hayman, that Johnny took a drink of whiskey the other day."

This wounded Mother deeply, and I was mortified. It was just a small drink, but to Mother, tasting whiskey was like losing your virginity. There was no way to do it just a little bit. She was hurt and disappointed in me.

I wondered why Mack did such a thing. The unwritten code among adolescents was never to tell on each other. I thought his tattling was retaliation for my beating him out of first chair in the band.

IN OCTOBER, AMERICAN TROOPS landed on Leyte Island in the Philippines. This was marvelous because the Japanese had humiliated us there thirty months earlier. Everyone thought the Battle of Leyte Gulf would shorten the war, and was happy that General McArthur had fulfilled his promise to return to the Philippines.

In Europe, some of our troops had crossed into Germany. We thought, perhaps, the war was almost over. Then, just before Christmas, the Germans started a surprise offensive in Belgium. It scared us and made us think maybe Hitler was making good on his boast to push us back in the ocean. Our hope now was in General Patton.

13

Dad had an old Philco radio in the back booth of the cafe, and he listened to commentators and war news and other serious things. I ate breakfast in the booth every school day and tuned in the Breakfast Club with Don McNeil. Once each show, their band played a march, and they "marched around the breakfast table." I loved the marches.

Dad wanted me to join him in listening to serious things on the radio and then discuss them. I wasn't too fond of this. I was getting to the age where parents seemed very old-fashioned and square. Dad was forty-five years older than me, and while I loved him, I thought he was ancient. Mostly I resisted, though I often joined him voluntarily for war news. He was a keen observer and could answer questions.

A day or two after New Year's in 1945, we were still concerned about the German offensive in Belgium.

I asked Dad, "Why are they calling it 'the Battle of the Bulge?'"

"If you look at a map," he explained, "the Allied lines stretch all across Europe from Holland to the south of France. The Germans knocked a small portion of the line backwards, and it looks like a bulge."

That made sense. I thought our country would straighten it out and turn the Germans back, but Dad explained we were caught by surprise. Fortunately General Patton broke through in a hurry and put the Germans in retreat. Because of this battle, the Germans didn't have a lot of resources left. Most everyone felt Hitler was crazy and the war would soon be over. Even some of his own generals tried to assassinate him. I understood things better, and I felt really good. You had to admit it, Dad was pretty smart.

Kenneth came walking in the cafe a few days later. The first thing, he said was, "I just ran into Maxine Ellison, and she had a letter from Billy. He's finished all of his training, and he's going to be assigned to a ship in the Pacific. That's just what he wanted. I bet he's really happy."

"That's kind of scary," Mother said. "There's a lot of fighting there."

Kenneth and I talked about Jemison things a while. He looked at Mother several times as if he had something to say and couldn't quite get it out.

Finally he managed. "Mrs. Hayman, I have something to tell you. I've decided I'm quitting school and joining the Navy."

"Why, you're not old enough," Mother answered. "You need your education."

Kenneth answered, "I hate school. I don't like studying, and I don't like the teachers. I'm sixteen, but everybody thinks I'm older. I talked to Henry and Mom, and they said they'd sign the papers."

"Now Kenneth," Mother admonished, "I'm not sure this is the right thing for you to do. I want you to think about it some more."

Kenneth answered, "Mrs. Hayman, my mind is made up. Billy Ellison and Reid Adams are in. I ought to be in, too."

A few days later Kenneth told us he convinced the recruiters he was seventeen and would be leaving soon. It made me sad, again, to see another friend leave.

LELAND WEST HAD GRADUATED the previous May, and I was now the first trumpet player. The Clanton cheerleaders had to swallow their pride and ask me to play "charge" for one of their yells. I wanted to be top man, but I hadn't anticipated one of the big benefits of the job. It made me the center of attention. This caused some of the girls to look my way and flirt.

I didn't know quite what to make of this. Louise Brown, my vision of pure Southern womanhood, was still my sweetie. The Jemison girls, who had gone to school with me for ten years, knew I was just a plump, harmless, shy teddy bear who could play the horn. The Clanton girls didn't know this. We Jemison folks gloried in our mastery of the band, but in our subconscious, we still thought of ourselves as country bumpkins and Clantonites as very sophisticated. The Clanton girls scared me. My hick ways were sure to make a fool of me. I didn't respond, with one exception. Leland West's sister Evelyn flirted, and I got a little friendly because I felt more comfortable with her. Louise noticed and let me know right away what she thought of it.

ALLIED TROOPS WERE SOON pushing into Germany from all sides, and it was obvious that Dad had been right. It was about over. We waited with great expectations for news that Germany had surrendered.

One afternoon in April, I went to the post office to get the mail. When I walked in, someone said, "Did you hear that Roosevelt died?" I was stunned; I couldn't believe it! I was fifteen years old, and this man had been president all of my life. I figured Franklin Delano Roosevelt would be president forever. Everybody mourned greatly. When we listened to his funeral on the radio, I couldn't keep from crying. I would have been embarrassed, but I noticed that everybody else was crying, too.

Newspaper reporters said awful things about the little Missouri farmer who replaced him. Harry Truman had the impossible job of following Franklin Delano Roosevelt. Many people never forgave him for it. Truman was vilified terribly, and I was with the rest in thinking there was no way he could fill the shoes of our lost hero.

Just two weeks later, on May 7, Germany surrendered. V-E Day had arrived at last, and everybody was exhilarated. We heard that Hitler had committed suicide, so Hirohito was the only one of the four evil demons still around. Mother commented that it was a shame President Roosevelt hadn't lived to share this moment. I thought so, too, and I shed another tear the next day when I read in the paper that "Roosevelt had given his life for the war effort, just like the soldiers on the battlefield."

BACK IN THE LATE '30s, people from the Department of Agriculture told Chilton County citizens that their sandy soil was more suited to peaches than to cotton. Some of the more progressive farmers put in peach orchards and proved the experts right. The peaches tasted great and sold well. Soon peach orchards popped up all around the county.

Dad thought maybe we could sell peaches in the cafe, so he planted an orchard on about four acres of our land. He would sometimes put me to work chopping weeds and spraying the peaches. The sprayer looked like a wheel-barrow with a tank and a manual pump. We'd mix up the spray and roll it out to the trees. I'd pump while Dad aimed the sprayer.

We grew good peaches. We'd pick them, pack them in baskets, and sell them in the cafe. Sometimes, at the height of the season, if we had more than we could sell in Jemison, Dad and I would remove the back seat of our 1933 Chevrolet and replace it with some boards. We could get several layers of peach baskets in the car. He and I would drive to Birmingham and peddle the peaches from door to door.

We were hauling load after load the early summer of 1945 and making a lot of money. I was fifteen years old, a pleasantly plump teenage boy with big blue eyes. I would take a basket of peaches, knock on a door, and ask the lady of the house if she would like to buy some. Dad went down the other side of the street. We kept going until we sold them all.

One day I knocked on a door, and when the lady opened it, she was in a house coat. She said, "Oh, you cute little boy! Come in." I went in, and she wanted to know what I was up to. I told her I was selling peaches. She said she'd buy two baskets. Then she said, "Sit down over here, and let me get you something to drink." I started getting nervous.

I'd heard stories from Tommy Sharp and others for several years, and with my experience taking the cows to Mr. Northcutt's bull, I had an idea of what could happen if I fell into the clutches of an older woman. I knew Dad would be looking for me, and the lady was getting more and more friendly. I didn't know what she had in mind, of course, but my imagination went into overtime. Just as she had the chocolate milk and cookies ready, I figured out an excuse to leave.

She said, "But surely you have time to eat what I've fixed. I just think you're a nice boy, and I want to be friendly."

She came over next to me, and my panic grew. "That's mighty nice, ma'am," I said, "but my Dad is real strict about the number of houses I have to call on. I'm really sorry, but if I don't leave right now I'll be in real big trouble."

I grabbed the front door, bolted out, and headed down the street. I forgot to collect the money for the two baskets of peaches she bought.

IN JULY, I WENT back to band camp at the University of Alabama. This camp band had about 120 members, and to my surprise, I was second chair in the twenty-two-person cornet section. Colonel Butler directed. Sometimes the first chair player would not be at practice, and I would play the cornet solos. Once after I had finished a solo, Colonel Butler stopped the band and said, "Did you all hear how beautifully this young man played?" My joy was complete.

The lead teacher for the cornets and trumpets was Eugene Jordan from Birmingham. He was band director at the Boys Industrial School and had ten children. One son was with Billy Graham's team and another played trombone with one of the big bands. One daughter was a brain surgeon and was with her husband in a foreign country doing mission work, and his daughter Irene was a Metropolitan Opera singer.

Mother and Dad came to the concert of the music camp band, and Mr. Jordan told them he would like to give me cornet lessons on Saturdays in Birmingham. This pleased Mother and Dad, and they agreed that we would find a way to begin lessons that fall.

THE DIXIE MUSIC CAMP, which drew students from several states, was held each summer at a college in Monticello, Arkansas. I wanted to go. Mom and Dad agreed because they wanted to buy an insurance policy on me which could only be written in Arkansas.

Two days before I left, I heard some terrible news—Louise Brown's family was moving to south Alabama. I rode to their house on my bicycle and said my teary good-byes to Louise. It was sad.

I arrived in Monticello and played before the judges. The band camp was large and had three bands: the really great one; the so-so one; and, the beginners. My ego took a terrible licking when I was placed about halfway down in the cornet section of the so-so band.

When band camp ended, I went to Brinkley to visit my step-grandmother and my Uncle J. L., who was just back from the Navy. Atom bombs were dropped on Hiroshima and Nagasaki while I was in Brinkley, and we all expected Japan would surrender at any moment.

J. L. and I were in the Rusher Hotel coffee shop one afternoon, and the radio was turned on. The announcer said, "We interrupt this program to bring you a message from the President of the United States." Harry Truman came on and announced that Japan had surrendered unconditionally.

Almost instantaneously, all of the sirens in Brinkley went off and people started blowing their automobile horns. J. L. and I ran out into the street. The fire station happened to be close by. They firemen brought out the fire engine with the siren going, and we jumped on the back of it and rode all over town. It was a wild and wonderful celebration.

SEYMOUR AND EDNA REYNOLDS came in the cafe for supper almost every day. They came other times for a cold drink, and they often ate lunch on weekends. They were among our best customers and friends. Mother and Edna were close allies in the Band Mothers, and this led to mutual support in other matters.

The Reynolds' jobs put them in contact with a wide variety of people. Seymour worked in construction, and Edna was in on everything that happened at school. When they came in the cafe, details on many interesting subjects were exchanged. This helped make the cafe a sort of intelligence center. Mary Edna and Annette were my good friends, and their musical skill helped maintain the ascendancy of Jemison in the band.

Edna was eating and talking. She took a bite of turnip greens, and started to chew. Then she stopped and sat silently with a puzzled look on her face. In a moment she reached in her mouth and pulled out a snail shell. She turned a pale shade of chartreuse and struggled to hold back a gag.

Mother saw that something was wrong and rushed over to the table. When she saw the snail shell and realized what happened, she was mortified. "Oh, Edna, I'm so sorry," she said. "We wouldn't have done that for the world."

Edna regained control, and she said with a weak smile, "It's all right. No harm done."

The incident was never mentioned again, and, since Edna did not like to cook, they remained our good customers and friends. They even ate the greens, but I noticed that Edna always poked around in them with her fork before she started. Dad didn't say anything, but he knew it was his fault. Thereafter, fresh turnip greens from the garden were examined and reexamined with a great deal more care.

DAD WOULD SEND ME periodically to the grist mill, which was by the gin and blacksmith shop on the other side of town. We would hitch Kit to the wagon and load it with corn cobs, corn stalks, a little corn, and a little bit of hay. I took along some tow-sacks, as we called them. Mr. McNeill would grind the material up and put it in the sacks. He would mix in just enough molasses to it more palatable.

I liked this chore. One of the great pleasures in life was to go when they were grinding corn and get a handful of the warm, fresh meal and eat it.

One day, Dad sent me with a load to the grist mill. Some other people were ahead of me, so I had to wait my turn. I was parked on the side of the dirt road by the mill. Suddenly, an Army bomber flew over about one hundred feet high. It made a terrible noise which startled me and everyone else and scared Kit. She started prancing and backing up. I hit her with the lines and yelled, but she just kept retreating.

The first thing I knew, the back wheels of the wagon went in a deep ditch beside the road, and part of the load slid out. Kit calmed down, but she couldn't move the wagon. Some of Mr. McNeill's helpers had to help me unload. When the wagon was empty, I stood to the side with the reins and urged Kit on while they lifted the back and pushed. We lifted the wagon back on the road, and I became the subject of some good-natured kidding. Everyone figured the bomber was piloted by Winston Davenport, who was from Jemison. Winston flew over every chance he had and was always several hundred feet below the legal limit.

JUNIOR CAME OVER ONE day toward the end of summer. "It's time to make a change," he said. "I'm going to Thorsby Institute this fall."

Thorsby Institute was run by the Congregational Church and was known for its good staff and academic excellence. I was stunned. I knew this was the end of our being in the band together and would certainly curtail our social activities. I also knew that Thorsby Institute was very expensive and Junior had no money. I questioned him about this.

"They're going to let me work," he explained. "I talked with the principal, Helen Jenkins, and I told her I needed a place to live. She said they'd take care of me. They have dormitories on campus, and I'll work as janitor in the church. I'll clean it every Sunday morning before church services and build a fire in the furnace. At 9:30 I'll ring the bell, then, I should have time to take a bath in my room and go to the 11 o'clock service. They'll pay me enough for books and spending money."

I couldn't believe what I was hearing; my buddy would no longer be down the street but three miles south. It was hard to digest.

After a while he said, "I've got something else to tell you. Mother invited us to visit her in Mobile. We can go down there on the bus. See if it's all right with your mother." Mother thought a lot of Ollie Dawson, so she said it was OK. A few days later, we were on our way.

We had a good visit in Mobile, and when we arrived home, Junior packed his bags and moved into the dorm at Thorsby Institute. School started a few days later, and I felt the loss. I thought a lot about him, his need for a place to live, and his need for a sense of belonging. I thought to myself, "I guess something really is missing if you don't feel like you belong to anyone."

SCHOOL STARTED, AND FOR the first time in my life I was really interested in college football. The two summers at music camp had made me a big fan of the Crimson Tide. Since 1920, Alabama was noted for its great teams, but I didn't know anything about it. Because of the war, they didn't play football in 1943. Now, most of Alabama's players were kids just out of high school. They happened to be a very talented group, and did well in spite of their youth. The stars of the other teams were off in the military.

Alabama's star was Harry Gilmer, and he was about the biggest sports hero Alabama ever had. He was to Alabama what Babe Ruth had been to the nation. Gilmer weighed only 160 pounds. He would jump-pass, he said, because he couldn't see over the linemen rushing in. He would jump up and throw the ball with great accuracy. I figured he could hit a squirrel in the eye at eighty yards.

I bought a little book called *This Is Harry Gilmer*, at a book store, and Harry himself was there to autograph it. It was almost more of a thrill than I could stand. The book presented Gilmer as an absolutely faultless idol, a person who never did wrong. It was full of pictures showing him throwing the ball and looking very serious. I read it and believed every word.

Since the war had just ended when the 1945 season started, few of the returning service men had made it back to college, and most teams were still playing their "war babies." Relative to the rest, Alabama's team was super good.

I was really into it. I followed every game and gloried in the team's achievements. They were undefeated and played Southern California in the Rose Bowl, which they won handily. Alabama had two All-Americans that year, Harry Gilmer and center Vaughn Manchu. Manchu was blind in one eye. I got to see them beat Mississippi State 55–0. The Million Dollar Band performed at the half, and I imagined myself marching with them in a pretty crimson and white uniform.

MARVIN HEADLY, ONE OF my good friends, assured me he was headed to Alabama, too. Marvin and I constituted the Jemison Lone Scout Patrol. We would walk back in the woods to a nice grassy spot by the creek. We would set up a tent and cook some bread and meat.

"Bucky" played the accordion, and he practiced hard to try to prove he was as musically talented as the people in the band. Occasionally, we would play a duet, but he always chose the music so that it was something which he knew well and I had to sight read. Naturally, he played better than I did.

Once, Bucky and I were out riding our bikes. We went to the baseball field beside the elementary school. We decided it would be fun if I rode on the back of his bicycle and give him instructions while he pedaled with his eyes closed. A man with a suitcase was walking across the field toward the highway, and we came pretty close to him. I told Bucky to go left when I meant right. He followed my instructions and ran right into the man.

"What the hell do you think you're doing?" the man demanded. His rage was obvious, and he was about to grab Bucky by the collar.

"But it wasn't my fault," Bucky tried to explain.

The man was within an ace of letting Bucky have it right in the nose, but he managed to hold his temper. He didn't buy Bucky's explanation that I really was the driver since it was obvious Bucky was the one "at the wheel."

Bucky kept trying to sputter an explanation, and the man finally made some insulting remark and walked away. I said not a word, but I enjoyed it immensely.

MOTHER AND OTHERS HAD started referring to me as a "young man." True, my body had reached adult proportions, but I couldn't get away from the feeling that I was still a child. There were reminders all around that it was time to be more mature. Billy, Kenneth, and Reid, who were not much older than I, had gone into the service. These were fellows I knew well. It was sobering to know they were in the war. It must be true that I was becoming a young man. Maturity beckoned, but I didn't know how to respond.

14

Bill Dubose, along with most of the men who had been in the service, came back to Jemison shortly after the war ended. When he walked into the cafe, Mother exclaimed, "Bill!" and rushed over to hug him. He shook hands with Coach Turner, Dad, and then with me.

"Wow, Johnny," he said to me, "you've certainly grown. You've become a man."

I beamed, wishing in my heart of hearts that I could be sure he was right.

"How was the Navy?" Coach asked.

"I can think of worse things," Bill answered, "but not a lot. Actually, I didn't have it so bad. They had me on a cruiser, escorting cargo ships across the north Atlantic. If you don't mind the meanest, coldest weather in the world, and staying seasick half the time, it's just like a fine cruise."

"Were you in any battles?" I asked with excitement.

"I'm afraid not," Bill said. "By the time I arrived, they had the U-boats under control. We had an alert every now and then when torpedoes were shot at the cargo ships. But mostly, it was just taking care of our ship."

We asked the usual questions about when he returned, and what he was going to do next. We asked if he was going to resume his chair business.

"I don't think so," Bill answered. "I had plenty of time to think while I was on the ship, and I've about decided it's time to give up inventing. I'll never make anything of it anyway, and I think good jobs will be easier to get now. I'm just going to lie around and rest a few days. Then I'll make up my mind."

We were all glad to have Bill back. He resumed his old habit of coming in the cafe two or three times a day, and he started talking to Dad about setting up a propane gas business. He figured propane and butane had a future now that people weren't so poor. He surmised it was easier to light a gas heater than to chop wood.

Billy Ellison came home and started back to school in my class. He had been two grades ahead of me before he went into the service. His life hadn't been as quiet as Bill's. He was on a battleship which supported troop landings the last few months of the war. He didn't say much about his experiences except, with bullets flying in every direction and Japanese suicide planes looking for ships to sink, it wasn't very glorious. He told us he ran into Kenneth Ray on the way home, and Kenneth told him he intended to stay in the Navy.

A few days before school started, we were all surprised when Joyce Howard, the Jemison basketball hero from the 1930s, walked in. Coach jumped up and grabbed Joyce's right hand with both of his. "How in the world are you doing?" he asked.

"I'm great!" Joyce said with a big smile. "Now that I'm out of the Army, my wife and I have decided to live in Jemison. We can use my aunt's house over by the Methodist church, and Lucille is going to teach English at the high school. She'll replace Miss Nichols." Miss Nichols, who had taught for decades, had retired. I found Joyce's story especially interesting because I would be in Mrs. Lucille's class.

SCHOOL WAS UNDER WAY soon, and I had reached the upper levels of high school society. I wasn't much of a lady's man and would go to almost any lengths to avoid a fist-fight. I was a good student and popular with the teachers. Most of all, I was the champion of the cornet in our little domain.

Early achievement on the cornet actually hurt my long-range prospects. My last three years in high school, no one in Jemison or Clanton dared challenge me, and I relaxed my efforts to improve. Most kids require competition to excel. I was probably the best ninth grade cornet player in Alabama, but state-wide, I gradually fell behind.

Junior went to Thorsby Institute and found the atmosphere to his liking. I didn't see him much anymore, though we remained friends. Neither he nor my family had a car.

I spent the weekend with him a few times, and I was impressed. His classmates seemed to be interested in books and culture, and they carried on intellectual conversations. Conversations among the boys in Jemison were never about such things, and the contrast made me think that the students at Thorsby Institute were very sophisticated.

While I was awed, I didn't want to go there. I had things made at Jemison High, and I wasn't about to give up my royal position with the horn.

Thorsby Institute regularly took its students to activities of the Birmingham Music Club. A few times Junior invited me to go with them, and Mother encouraged it in hopes I would move beyond Ernest Tubb and Roy Acuff. The trips were fun. I got to see Arthur Rubinstein, the Minneapolis Symphony, and "Carmen" performed by the Metropolitan Opera. To my surprise, I sort of liked it.

EARLY THE FALL OF my junior year, Mother took me to Birmingham to buy some clothes. I needed a light jacket, and while Mother preferred to be a little reserved in choosing colors, I saw a bright crimson jacket I just had to have. It reminded me of the Crimson Tide. Mother finally relented and let me have it. The bright color, however, produced some unexpected consequences.

For example, I wore it when we went to the State Fair in Birmingham that fall. Mother and Evie went in one direction, and James Lester and I went in another. There were all sorts of enticing hoochie-coochie shows up and down the midway, so James Lester and I decided we would sneak in one. We looked carefully to be sure no one was watching, and in we went.

On the way home, we talked for a while about the wonders of the fair. Then Mother gave Evie a wink and asked, "How did you boys like the dancing girls in that show?"

James Lester and I both turned the color of my jacket. We were obviously caught, so there was no use trying to deny it. I asked, "How did you know about that?"

"It was easy," Mother answered. "We were on the other side of the midway, but we saw your coat."

A FEW MONTHS LATER I went to the district basketball tournament in Selma with a group of older boys from school who were veterans. Between the afternoon and night games they suggested we take a little ride and look at the town. We drove around a bit, and they pulled up at a place on the edge of town. It was a little shabby looking, and I wasn't sure what it was. The older boys suggested we go in for a Coke.

On the inside were some booths and a long counter with stools. A group of young girls in skimpy clothing sat on the stools, and I thought it was kind of strange they were in there by themselves. I sat on a stool and ordered a Coke. In a minute one of the girls walked up to me. "That's a mighty purty red coat you got on thar," she said.

"I'm glad you like it," I answered, a little surprised that she spoke when she didn't know me.

"How much would ya take for hit?" she asked.

"I guess I'd better keep it," I said. "My mother bought it for me, and she wouldn't like me losing it."

"I sure wouldn't want to get between you and your ma," the girl answered, "but tell ya what. I usually charge a purty penny for my services, but I'll trade ya even if you'll give me that coat."

Suddenly it occurred to me what was going on. The other boys were in the corner bending over with laughter. They had put one over on me. They had deliberately brought me to a house of ill repute. I went into panic, but I managed to say, "You're very nice, ma'am, and that's an interesting thought, but I've got to be going." I headed for the car in a hurry. The others followed, still laughing big and enjoying themselves immensely.

Every time I wore the red coat to school the next few weeks, people would snicker and ask me how much I thought it was worth.

CARS WERE IMPOSSIBLE TO buy during the war because all production went into war materials. After the war ended, the car manufacturers changed back to civilian vehicles as soon as they could, but the wait list was long. If a person didn't have the right connections, he had to put his name on a waiting list, and it could take a year or more to get a car.

We had been without a car more than a year, and it was very inconvenient. Mother and Dad hadn't realized it would take so long to get a new one when they sold the '33. Our name was on a lot of lists, but time dragged on with no car.

One of our customers was Tom Wood, president of the Wood Chevrolet dealership in Birmingham. He went to Montgomery often, and was in the habit of stopping in the cafe on most of his trips. In the course of our conversations, he learned about our automobile situation. Mother did not ask to be on a list at his company because she didn't want him to think she would try to take advantage of his friendship. I wasn't sure I followed her logic.

One day, just before Thanksgiving, Tom Wood was in the cafe eating a piece of pie. I walked in, and he said, "Tell me, Johnny, what kind of a car do you like?"

"I like 'em all," I answered. "The way things are right now, I'd settle for anything."

"What did y'all use to have?" he inquired.

"A 1933 Chevrolet," I said.

"What do you think about the 1947 Chevrolets?" he asked.

"Ooh, they're really something!" I responded.

Mother was standing on the other side of the counter. She wasn't paying close attention until his next sentence.

"Tell your mother," he said, "that there is a pretty two-tone car in our lot which looks like it was made for y'all."

Mother looked at him very excited. "Do you mean what I think you mean?" she asked.

"Yes," he said with a big smile. "I've been thinking about y'all. The other day a really nice-looking car came in, and I told our service manager to set it aside. You can have it if you want it."

She looked at me in mock seriousness. "Do you think we ought to get it?"

"Yes, yes, yes!!" I shouted, hardly daring to believe my ears.

The next Tuesday, Mother and I rode the Greyhound bus to Birmingham and took a taxi to Wood Chevrolet. All of the papers were signed, and we were led to a beautiful new car. It was light tan on the bottom and green on the top. I thought it was the most beautiful car I had ever seen.

EARLY IN DECEMBER, SOMETHING was wrong with old Babe, our tender-hearted cow. She started moping around, and it was clear she didn't feel well. Dad called a young Auburn graduate, a veterinarian from Thorsby, Thomas Hayes.

Thomas looked at Babe, and he couldn't quite figure out her problem. He tried some medicine. He came back the next afternoon to check, and she wasn't any better. He thought about it some more and gave her some different meds. Alas, she just seemed to get worse. She broke my heart pleading with those big sad eyes for me to help, but I didn't know what to do.

The next Friday night, we were in the house listening to *Lum and Abner* on the radio. Suddenly there was a loud knock on the door. When Mother opened it, there stood Thomas Hayes. He looked very bright-eyed and said, "I've figured out what's wrong with the cow!"

We went to the barn, and there in her favorite stall, Babe lay dead. Thomas Hayes looked dejected, apologized profusely, and drove away.

It was almost 11 p.m., and I didn't see any harm in leaving her there until morning. Dad had other ideas about it. He told me to put on a coat and come with him. It was crispy cold. Mother asked, "What are you going to do?"

"We going to bury the cow," Dad answered.

"But why do you have to do it now," Mother asked. The same question was on my mind.

"If we don't do it now, she will bloat up, and it will affect the other cows," Dad answered. Neither of us knew enough about animals to dispute him, so out we went.

We caught Kit easily. Since it wasn't morning, and she wasn't expecting to have to do anything until well after sunrise, she was right by the barn. We put the harness on her, but instead of hitching her to the plow, Dad rigged up some ropes on the harness and attached them to old Babe. He used Kit to drag Babe to the back side of the pasture. Kit tried to protest, but Dad used his mule attitude changer to get her cooperation.

Dad brought along a shovel, and he had me dig a deep hole. It had to be big so Babe would fit. I dug and dug, and it was well past 3 a.m. before the hole was big enough. Dad kept Kit hitched up so she could pull Babe in. Kit was real spooked by the whole thing and kept shifting from side to side, her eyes wide open and her ears sticking straight up. Finally, Dad nudged Kit to drag Babe into the hole. When Dad saw everything was all right, he said, "Take Kit to the barn and let her go. Then get the other shovel and come back out here."

I took Kit back to the barn, removed the harness and the bridle, and released her. Kit headed as fast as she could for the best hiding spot she knew.

We covered Babe and filled up the hole. We packed it hard on top, and Dad left a pile to the side because he knew the hole would sink as Babe disintegrated.

We really felt bad about Babe, and Mother kept trying to assure Thomas Hayes it was all right. It didn't hurt much financially because, shortly after the war ended, the state health department decided to protect the public from people like us who sold fresh milk. Rules were passed that required milking stalls with concrete floors and running water connected to hoses for washing everything down. It cost too much for us to do, so Mother started buying her milk products.

BARBARA DID WELL AT Auburn. She rode home with someone from Chilton County every two or three weeks, so we saw a lot of her. In everyone's eyes, she was now in the adult world, and she spent more time talking to Mother than to me.

One weekend when she was home, the four of us were sitting together in the cafe. During a lull, Barbara said, "I think it's time I tell you I've met a boy at Auburn that I like very much."

Mother paused a moment, while Dad and I both watched at full attention. She proceeded to tell us his name was Jesse James.

"Jesse James!" Dad said with a big laugh, unable to contain himself. "I thought they did away with him fifty years ago. Where in the world did you find Jesse James?"

Barbara blushed and acted a little aggravated. Mother gave Dad a signal with her eyes to be quiet. "We want to hear all about it, dear. Tell us about him."

"Well, he grew up in Florence, and worked as a waiter in my dorm's dining hall. He graduated with a degree in electrical engineering last spring, and he's coming back this year for a second degree in engineering physics.

This is a new degree that Auburn has started offering."

That sounded pretty potent. Dad and I were impressed.

The discussion continued, and it was decided we would meet Jesse in Birmingham. The next Saturday, we put on our nice clothes and drove in our new car to Birmingham. At the appointed place and time, a young man came walking up. He had a crew cut and to me, he could have been a twin to Spike Jones, the orchestra director whose group played crazy music.

Introductions were made. Jesse looked at me. "So you're John. Barbara's told me all about you. She says you think you want to go to the University of Alabama, but we're going to change that."

My smile turned to a hard frown. "Wrong, wrong, wrong," I thought. The others just laughed, and we headed to a cafeteria for lunch. With me, Jesse James had started on the wrong foot.

Mother and Dad liked him, and soon he was driving to Jemison from Auburn every few weeks. I could tell that he and Barbara were getting thicker and thicker.

MR. BURTON RESIGNED AS band director and was replaced by Maurice Brausa, who had just returned from the service. Mr. Brausa was more pleasant that Mr. Burton, so we all liked him.

He had to take things as he found them in the band, and he started spending lots of time in Jemison. He had an Army surplus jeep, and I thought that was pretty neat. He began to stop regularly at the cafe. Soon we all became great friends.

Mr. Brausa was something of a character. He lived alone in an apartment in Clanton, and we soon heard rumors that his garbage container was filled with beer cans when it was emptied. Chilton County was dry, and most people were more discreet with their beer cans.

Mother kidded him about it one day, and he said, "Nothing wrong with a little beer. It helps me think up these complicated drills we do at football games."

As we got to know Mr. Brausa, he told us he was married but his wife lived in Pensacola, Florida. I wanted to know about that arrangement, but Mother would not let me pursue it.

I had been taking cornet lessons from Mr. Jordan since the previous fall. Mother arranged for me to ride to Birmingham and back with a local merchant who drove to a wholesale house each week. He dropped me off in downtown Birmingham, and I rode the street car to the east side of town where the Jordans lived. I really liked the street cars.

Mr. Jordan and his wife were always friendly with me. They would stop in the cafe and eat when they were driving south from Birmingham. Several times he had me spend the night with them and play with the Boys Industrial School Band the next day. Since the boys were in the school for some kind of disciplinary problem, Mother and Dad had mixed emotions about it.

I wasn't making the progress I should have. No one challenged my position in the band, and I didn't practice as much anymore. Now that I was in the upper reaches of high school life, Dad had given up trying to get me to work in the garden. He and Jack Sales did it and let me go my way.

LUCILLE HOWARD WAS MY English teacher that year. She was red-headed and attractive, and she was full of energy and good cheer. Everybody liked her. She always smiled, and in her way, she managed to get students to learn more English than the teachers who seemed to take things so seriously.

Mrs. Howard persuaded Mr. Peterson to let her teach French. It was the first time a foreign language had been taught at Jemison High. Joe and I were among the students, and Joe outdid me. Somehow, French wasn't my thing.

A few months after school started, we began hearing rumors that Bill Dubose was getting thick with one of the teachers, Lera Dee Conway. She was our dentist's daughter and a graduate of Alabama College in Montevallo. Bill had started Central Alabama Gas Company, was doing well, and obviously a good catch

Bill was forty years old, and Lera Dee was twenty-five. We were not sure her parents would approve of this relationship. Apparently they did, because Bill and Lera Dee announced their wedding plans for the coming December.

MR. BRAUSA REALLY DID good things with the band. Everybody liked him, and he brought in new music. He had played a baritone horn in college, and he still practiced regularly. Sometimes he would play a solo between acts of a play or at some other occasion. He had great technique and produced a beautiful sound.

Since his wife was in Pensacola, he didn't have anything to do nights and week-ends except practice his horn and drink beer, so he started spending a lot of time in the cafe.

One Sunday afternoon, he said to Mother, "Mrs. Hayman, do you think the people here would enjoy a little classical music in our next concert?"

"I don't know," Mother answered. "It depends on how it sounds. Just don't tell anyone it's classical, and they won't know the difference. Except for Junior Dawson, not many folks around here are familiar with that kind of music."

Mr. Brausa laughed. "You're right, but if it sounds pretty, maybe they will like it. I was thinking maybe I'd try a clarinet quartet by Bach, and I think our players could handle it. I also thought I would get Johnny to play a solo and have Lamar Deloach play a trombone solo. Ann Turner, Annette, and Mary Edna could play, and that little Groom boy from Clanton could take the fourth part."

The four players started practicing, and the music was more complex than anything before. One or two would play for a considerable time, and the others would have to count carefully so they would know when to come in. They kept getting lost during practice, and Mr. Brausa kept trying to teach them how to keep up with their place. As the concert approached, he started getting uneasy, but he decided to go ahead with it because he thought Ann could keep the others together.

The night of the concert came. The band was sounding good. By then, we could handle Sousa marches and play pieces of medium difficulty like the *Light Cavalry Overture*. I planted my feet, pushed my sleeves back, got set for serious business, and played my solo.

After the intermission, we opened with a rousing march. The clarinet quartet was next. Jemison was about to be introduced to something serious. The four clarinet players sat in the front of the band, two on each side, and Mr. Brausa sat in front of them. As they went along, the little Groom boy (Joe) got lost. His efforts to find his place spread confusion among the rest, and soon they were in a hopeless tangle.

Mr. Brausa, in obvious exasperation, made a sweeping gesture to stop
them, and then in a voice clearly audible in the back of the auditorium,
he said, "Section B, damn it." They managed to finish without total catas-
trophe. People in Jemison were amused by it, though they said nothing
and just gave compliments to all of us. Nobody ever told them it was their
introduction to classical music.

AS THE SPRING PROGRESSED, I started hearing whispers about this big party
the boys were planning to have at Ballard's pond. I was a little perturbed
because nobody mentioned it to me. I wasn't the greatest lady's man in the
crowd, but I was always included in the parties.

I could tell the time for their occasion was getting close, and one day I
cornered Mack and asked, "What's this I hear about a party?"

"We're having one two weeks from Friday night at Ballard's pond," he
answered.

"Why haven't I been invited?" I demanded.

"We just didn't think you'd want to come," he said.

"I don't know where you got that idea. I'm always asked to go to the
parties, and I always go."

"But Johnny," he said, getting close and talking in my ear in a whisper.
"It's a sex party."

I was stunned and walked away. I was highly insulted. What made them
think I wouldn't want to go to a sex party, just because I was secretary of the
Sunday School at the Baptist Church? Who did they think they were? The
more I thought about it, the madder I became. Meanwhile, I could see the
boys giggling and whispering to each other in little groups.

Marvin Headley had enrolled at the University of Alabama that fall. He
was home the next weekend, and I told him about it.

"Do you really think they'll do such a thing?" I asked.

"You never know," Marvin answered. "Some of them sure make a lot
of big talk."

We decided we would spy on them. Marvin borrowed a couple of pairs
of binoculars. At the appointed hour, we sneaked in the back way through
Dr. Ballard's pasture and crept up to some bushes at the top of the hill.

About twenty of the town's "prized" youth were gathered around a campfire.

We could see them clearly, and we waited in great anticipation. They roasted wieners and seemed to be having a good time. But nothing out of the ordinary appeared to be happening.

Finally, about 11 p.m., they walked to their cars, and the boys drove the girls home. I sat there for a few minutes puzzled.

After the last couple left, I said "Why, they didn't have a sex party at all."

Marvin said, "I expect it's like all the other smart talk about their conquests. They smart off and try to outdo each other bragging, but it's just baloney. I guess they forgot one little detail—the girls didn't know what the party was supposed to be about."

15

When people in Jemison wanted to meet and talk, they came to the cafe. The fact it was run by someone as rock solid as Edith Hayman gave Jemison something most other towns its size didn't have.

Sunday lunch (dinner we called it) was our biggest single event of the week. The ladies of Jemison didn't want to cook after church, and their husbands were easily persuaded to eat out. Mother and her helpers worked hard from 7:30 a.m. to get ready, and were very busy during the two-hour rush which started about noon.

Occasionally, I helped wait on tables after getting home from church, but Mother didn't want me to soil my Sunday clothes. So my regular job was to handle the cash register. This was a pleasant duty because I could listen to all of the talk. Also, I prided myself on my ability to handle complicated transactions in my head, like when a family had two plate lunches, two hamburgers, a toasted cheese, a barbecue, and a variety of drinks. Seymour, Edna, Mary Edna, and Annette Reynolds were always among the customers for Sunday lunch. They went home after church to remove some of their finery and came to the cafe a little after 1 o'clock. They finished lunch about the time the rush was ending and were the first of the Sunday afternoon leisurely-talk crowd. Every conceivable subject was covered. The pleasant conversation continued until supper time approached.

A FEW DAYS AFTER school ended in May 1947, Mother asked me, "When is band camp this year?"

"It's at the end of June, I think, but I'm not going."

"Not going!" Mother exclaimed. "But what about Colonel Butler, and Mr. Jordan, and the University?"

"Well, they're exciting," I said, "but I want to go to summer school and take advanced algebra. There are other things I want to take during the regular school year, and I want to get algebra out of the way."

Mother was puzzled, but she accepted what I said. I had told only a small part of the truth, however. The real reason I wanted to go to summer school was that I didn't want to take advanced algebra from Miss Harvey.

I was going to be a senior, and for fifteen years Miss Harvey had been senior class sponsor. She had a habit of making one of the senior boys her pet. She fawned over them and openly favored them in school. This was a big joke to the students. I figured it was best not to give Miss Harvey the chance to make me her pet. My caution was unnecessary, as it turned out, because Mack was already the apple of her eye.

I went to summer school in Clanton, and to my surprise, my teacher was Miss Harvey! Most of the other students were from Clanton, and I knew a lot of them through the band, so it was fun. We even had a couple of picnics, and I noticed a really cute girl named Mary Clyde Mims. I was friendly, and she was friendly right back. One of her friends told me that she had all kinds of suitors in Clanton, but being a musician, she admired my cornet playing. "Hmmmm," I thought. "Maybe I better get back to practicing."

ONE PLEASANT AFTERNOON IN early summer, Edna was in the cafe, and she asked Mother, "What's this I hear about Barbara? Is she getting serious?"

Mother confirmed Edna's suspicions. Barbara was graduating at the end of the summer term, and her plans were to marry after that. Mother and Dad had hoped Barbara would work a year or two and get some experience before she married, but Barbara had other ideas. Barbara had told them, "No arguments, please."

A few days later, Mother received a letter from Barbara saying she would be home the next weekend to start planning for the big event. So things went into high gear in Mother's mind. Barbara said she and Jesse didn't want a church wedding. They just wanted a quiet ceremony in our living room. The wedding date was set to take place about a month after graduation. On a Thursday night late in August, we drove to Auburn to see Barbara awarded the Bachelor's degree in Secretarial Science. Jesse James had finished his second degree in June, and was working at Southern Research in Birmingham.

Barbara rode home to Jemison with us, and there was a mad flurry for the next few weeks. Mother and Barbara managed to get everything ready. On the wedding day, Jesse showed up with his parents and best man. The wedding went off without a hitch, and after some punch and considerable kidding, the newlyweds drove off in Jesse's new second-hand car. Mother was all teary-eyed again, but this time I understood a little better.

MR. PETERSON HAD RELENTED and Jemison was finally going to have a football team. Heavy pressure had been put on the county Board of Education by some influential Jemison citizens. Every other school had a team, and Jemison wanted one, too, Mr. Peterson's fear that it was too dangerous was not taken into account. A new football field was built with hard clay. Alton Cobb, who had never played football, was appointed coach.

Bill didn't visit the cafe nearly as often as he had before his Navy days. He was busy running his successful butane/propane gas business. Coach commented one day that things were certainly different. The G. I. Bill of Rights was paying for veterans' education, times were good, and so were the opportunities. Even the current president of the senior class, Robert Hall, was a Navy veteran.

Robert enjoyed life and his easy-going manner was very appealing. He was being recruited for the football team. Much to the chagrin of Jemison, Robert announced he was going out for the cheerleading squad instead. The Jemison folks could not understand how a Navy veteran, who was part of the amphibious force at Iwa Jima and Okinawa, would go out for cheerleading. Robert just commented that cheerleading beat the heck out of crawling up on a beach in front of invasion troops.

True to his word, Robert went out for cheerleader. The football team had Joe Bratton at center, Billy Ellison at quarterback, and Mack Smith at half back. I was larger than most boys my age, and the others thought I could help with the line. I started to go out for football, but Mr. Brausa persuaded me that my lips were too valuable to risk.

Miss Harvey was the cheerleading sponsor. Mother asked Robert how Miss Harvey was doing as cheerleading sponsor. This was all new to Jemison.

"Well, we were practicing the other day, and Miss Harvey was sitting on one of those little benches by the football field. Norris Vickery was showing out, and he jumped up on the bench. It flipped over, and Miss Harvey went flying. There she lay with her skirt up high and her legs spread apart. She couldn't get up. I wanted to help her, but I couldn't do anything but laugh. I said, 'Lordy, here's Christmas.'"

That got a great laugh from everyone in the cafe, and even Mother couldn't keep from smiling. "But what I want to know," she said, "is whether y'all are helping the football team."

"We're trying mighty hard," Robert said. "They haven't won a game yet, but they keep acting more like a football team. We expect we'll be able to beat Isabella."

Coach, who had just walked in, smiled. "We're mighty glad Jemison started a team," he said. "Now we have a breather on our schedule."

A WEEKLY TOPIC IN the cafe was the progress of the new football team. They kept playing better each week, and they kept having close, but losing, games. Everybody was pointing toward Isabella. The week before that game, Jemison played a strong Centerville team and lost by just one touchdown. Hopes were soaring.

The Isabella game was played at their field on a Friday afternoon in late October. It had to be in the afternoon because Isabella didn't have lights. I couldn't go because I had a dental appointment. When I got home, we all sat in the cafe waiting with bated breath for the Jemison crowd to return.

Soon a car pulled up, and out came Billy, Mack, and Reid. As they walked in, we could tell by their faces that the news wasn't good. The three of them sat at the counter, and Mother walked out and stood in front of them, "Tell us about it."

"Well, Mrs. Hayman," Billy answered, "we played the hardest and the best so far, but Coach Turner really had his team up for this game."

"Those Isabella boys have never played like that," Mack chimed in. "It was so close, and we were doing so good. We were six points ahead with only two minutes to go. Then they got the ball and started down the field. They scored with just a few seconds left, kicked the extra point, and beat us by one."

HALLOWEEN CAME THE NEXT Tuesday, and two days later a crowd was in the cafe after school talking about the prospects for Friday's game against Columbiana. Isabella had taken away our confidence, but everybody was still putting up a brave front.

Isabella's loss was not enough to curb the Halloween mischief in Jemison. Billy Ellison decided he would share the details of the biggest prank. "Well, several of us went up to Mr. Peterson's house to do a little Halloween mischief. Some wanted to throw a two-by-four through his window, but I said, 'No, we can't do anything like that. Let's just play a little joke on him.'"

"Somebody had a ball of twine, and we decided to tie one end of it to the handle on his screen door. Then we went across the road to that little ditch. I went back and knocked on his door, and I ran to the ditch before he got there. He came to the door and looked all around, and when he couldn't see anything, he went back in. We'd pull the string and slam the door. Mr. Peterson would come back out and look, but he never could figure out what was happening. We were laughing and having a big time, and we went on with it for a half-hour or so. He never did notice the string."

Most of the football team was in on the trick. It was a good Halloween stunt, but their imagination didn't help on Friday night. They lost the game to Columbiana, and the next week they lost the last game of the year to Maplesville. Jemison ended its first football season with a record of no wins and eight losses.

The first annual Jemison High School Football Banquet was held early in December, and Robert Hall was the master of ceremonies. "Let's all give a cheer," he said. "Our glorious team lost every game, but they never lost the will to win. They fought all the way."

A FEW DAYS BEFORE Christmas, Coach Turner's elderly mother-in-law, who lived with the Turners, died. In Jemison in 1947, the viewing was still held in the living room of the family home.

A group was in the living room about 10 o'clock the night before the funeral, and I heard someone say that there wasn't anyone to stay with the corpse that night. I didn't know why someone had to stay up with the corpse, but it was the custom.

I spotted Mary Edna on the other side of the room, and I walked over. "What are you doing tonight?" I asked.

"I'm going home, of course," she answered. "What kind of a question is that?"

"They don't have anybody to stay up with the body," I responded.

"That's too bad," Mary Edna said.

"I dare you to stay here with me," I said.

Mary Edna looked me straight in the eye. She wasn't one to dodge a challenge. "You don't dare me. I'll stay here if you will."

I announced to Coach Turner that Mary Edna and I would handle the overnight duties.

"Are you sure?" he asked. "It's a long time from midnight to dawn."

"Don't you worry about a thing," I assured him. "We'll take care of it."

Both of our parents were in the room, and while they doubted the wisdom of it, they agreed to let us stay.

Everybody went home shortly after 11, and about midnight Coach and his family retired. Mary Edna and I sat on a couch on one side of the room, and the coffin with the lid open was on the other side. We avoided turning our eyes in that direction and kept up an animated but quiet conversation.

Coach was right. It was a long night, and time seemed to really drag after 2:30. Mary Edna was a big talker, and she kept going strong right through the wee hours.

The heat had been turned down in the house, and as the temperature changed, the casket creaked. About 3 o'clock, it popped really big. Mary Edna and I both jumped, and she looked at me with big eyes. "What was that?" she asked.

For the first time since our caper started, I looked long and hard directly at the casket. I wanted to make sure the deceased hadn't decided to come back to life. Everything seemed in order. In a quiet voice I answered, "I guess it was just the coffin reacting to the temperature."

Secretly, we both thought this wasn't such a good idea, but neither of us would have admitted it. By 4 o'clock, we were both digging into our resources and straining our brains to the limit to keep the talk going. Dawn finally came, the deceased was still quietly in her place, and neither Mary Edna nor I had thought once about being sleepy. Our anxiety eased with the early light, and soon Coach came in and told us what a great deed we had done.

As we walked home, Mary Edna asked me, "Do you feel like we did a really good deed?"

"No," I said. "I feel more like a big coward than a do-gooder. What about you?"

"Me, too," she said. "I guess the difference is just the way other people look at what you've done."

THE BAND MOTHERS CLUB had managed an informal non-aggression agreement and met in the cafe once a month. Mother and Mrs. Smith had buried their respective hatchets. The band kept getting a little better as the Jemison contingent matured. Some of the Clanton kids started practicing seriously to see if they could end their humiliation, but we had the top positions firmly in hand, a situation that only time and graduation would relieve.

The state band contest was held in Tuscaloosa each year on the University of Alabama campus. During my senior year, our thirty-two members attended, happy for the chance to stay overnight away from home.

We were in the middle-sized school division, and when it came our turn to play, we were almost lost on the stage. The band before us had 110 members, and our first task was to get all of their chairs out of the way. We played the music we had practiced, and then came the most terrifying of all contest experiences, sight-reading a piece. Mr. Brausa struggled mightily and pulled us through it, and somehow we all finished about the same time.

When the results were announced, our band won first place in the middle division. The band with 110 members complained that it wasn't fair because our band was actually made up of players from two schools. The complaint was ignored. Everyone in Jemison was very proud of us, even though we wore Clanton's orange and blue on that occasion.

The next Sunday, Mr. Brausa came up to the cafe early and had a great day receiving congratulations from everyone who came in. I asked him if he wanted to go to Baptist Training Union with me that night, and he did.

After that, he went to church with me regularly on Sunday nights. None of us had any illusions that religion was penetrating his soul. He was just lonely and liked the companionship.

JEMISON HAD A GOOD basketball team that year. Mack was the best player, and he was ably supported by Billy and Reid.

My job at basketball games was to keep score, and Joe kept time. The other team also had a scorekeeper and a timekeeper. Rumor had it among opposing teams that, depending on the situation, games at Jemison might be a few seconds shorter or a few seconds longer than the rules allowed.

I hadn't missed a game in three years, but the night Jemison was to play Marbury on their court, I had an unsolvable conflict. The Million Dollar Band was giving a concert at Montevallo, a few miles away, and I just couldn't miss that. So they arranged for a substitute scorekeeper.

Joe was only supposed to observe, but when the Marbury timekeeper didn't show up, they asked him to take over because of his experience. Marbury had lost only one game that year, to Jemison, on our court. They were figuring on revenge. The game was very close. It came down to the last few seconds. Marbury was ahead by one point. Our coach called time out, and the Marbury coach came over to see how many seconds were left. There were too many, in his opinion. Jemison took the ball and scored immediately, and just as Marbury threw it in, Joe blew the whistle to end the game.

The Marbury crowd was incensed, and some of their toughies grabbed Joe. A fight broke out, and it soon turned into a general riot. Jemison was about to be murdered. The Maplesville team came along on their way home from a game, and when they saw what was happening, they stopped and helped Jemison escape.

When we heard about it the next morning, we were told that Joe was in bad shape. Apparently, he was covered in blood and was moaning when they took him home. Just as we were getting ready to plan a wake, Joe came bounding in the cafe with a big grin on his face.

"We heard you were in terrible shape," I said. "What happened?"

"What does it look like? I'm fine." he responded. "You really missed a good one."

"But what about all the blood we heard about?"

"It wasn't my blood," he said. "Why do you think I wear those big Brogan shoes?"

Jemison had lost only three games when the season ended, and two of the losses were to Isabella. Coach Turner had a super good team which was seeded first in the district tournament. As the draw would have it, Jemison wound up in the same bracket with Isabella. Each team won its first game, and then came the big one. It was Jemison against Isabella. Everybody went to Selma to see it. The score went back and forth, with Jemison hanging in pretty good. With about five minutes to go, Mack Smith suddenly started hitting shots from all angles. Jemison won the game by eight points. Mack was the hero, and Coach had to put up with our kidding for several months.

A COUPLE OF DAYS after the game, a large group gathered in the cafe, celebrating and reliving the glory. The Reynolds, Bill and Lera Dee, and Miss Harvey were there. So were Mack, Billy, and Reid from the basketball team. Annette and Mary Edna were present, along with Ann Turner, Mary Julia Blewster, and Robert Hall. Mary Julia and Robert had been dating regularly, and we all suspected things might be getting serious.

Mack was the hero of the game, and he basked in his glory. Billy kept the crowd laughing with his funny remarks. Robert sat to the side, a confident smile on his face, his status as leader of the high school group unquestioned.

Without any prompting, the group became nostalgic, and started telling stories and talking about what a wonderful place Jemison was to live. Mary Julia decided to lighten things up a bit, and, with a big grin on her face, stated, "And Mrs. Hayman serves the world's greatest hamburgers. One of my dreams is to eat all the cafe's hamburgers and GooGoo Clusters I can eat."

Everybody laughed. They all certainly understood about the hamburgers, but they wanted to know why the GooGoo Clusters. Mary Julia solved the mystery.

"Back before we had any money, I used to eat in the lunch room at school. I ate what was served and glad to get it. Barbara Jean Price always sat on the other side of the table from me. After she ate her lunch, she ate a GooGoo Cluster she had brought for dessert. Our lunch only cost five cents a day, but those GooGoos cost ten cents each. Nobody else could afford one. Ever since then, I've craved GooGoo Clusters."

Everyone laughed. We had warm feelings for our town and for our friends. There was no question; it was a good life.

16

Almost before we knew it, the end of our senior year in high school was upon us. My classmates and I, at least those who were not veterans, were still trying to figure out what being an adult meant. To the younger students, however, our ignorance about such things didn't matter. Seniors were the elite.

It had been a fun year. I had a light schedule because I had taken advanced algebra in summer school, and had already taken all of the science courses offered at Jemison. The subject I liked best that year was typing, especially since Bill Dubose's wife was my teacher. I also knew I needed typing because I faced many term papers in college. Somehow, my fingers just naturally fit the keys, and I could fly right from the start.

This led to another opportunity. The teachers decided Jemison High School should have a weekly newspaper. They named Mrs. Dubose as sponsor. When she asked for volunteers in her typing classes to help with the newspaper, five of us stepped forward—four girls and me. I was elected editor. Francis Hubbard, the second fastest typist, won the contest for naming the paper, and became associate editor. The paper was named *The Panthergram*.

The paper was great fun. I wrote what I thought were high-sounding editorials. Billy Ellison was sports editor and put his humor into game stories. Robert Hall contributed pieces consistent with his status as student leader. Francis and the girls made sure the female perspective was covered.

Being on the paper staff added to my typing skills; I could quickly finish the class assignments then use the typewriter for advancing my creative skills, such as typing Christmas trees and other designs. It didn't help my typing class popularity.

ALL THE TEACHERS LIKED and trusted me. They figured I was going to get an A, so that came about without much effort on my part. I learned later that the attitude which resulted was not suited to higher education, but it was fun while it lasted.

I volunteered for every extra assignment. I became the stage manager, and I handled the lighting at all of the plays and activities. This required some preparation, of course, and got me out of class. I learned to operate the motion picture projector and helped anyone who wanted to use it. I ran errands for Mr. Peterson and for the teachers.

As a result, I was out of class a good bit of time. The teachers didn't ask why because they figured I was doing something worthwhile. The other boys couldn't resist sneaking off sometimes and playing hooky, and they got in trouble. If I wanted to go somewhere, I just walked out the front door, and nobody paid any attention. I was sure there was a moral in this situation, but I've never been able to figure it out.

I HADN'T SEEN MUCH of Junior. He graduated from high school the previous spring, and headed off to college without saying much to anybody. At Thanksgiving he was back in Jemison, and he came by to talk.

After graduating from Thorsby Institute with honors, he decided he wanted to go to the University of Alabama. He talked with his dad, hoping his dad would help with tuition. His dad became irritated, and told Junior that if he wanted to go to college, fine, but not to count on him for support. Junior was disappointed.

"I was feeling very bad about it, and I came to the cafe. I told your mother what I wanted to do and what had happened; she was very supportive and encouraged me to go on to college. If I needed it, she said, she would loan me some money. That was just what I needed to hear. I went on to Tuscaloosa the first of June and got a job at a restaurant. I'm earning money and getting my food."

Mother had never told the story about the loan offer.

By the time the fall quarter started, Junior had saved enough to pay his tuition. He also met with the Dean of Students and told him about his economic plight. The dean helped Junior get a better paying job, and Junior felt more optimistic about getting through school.

When I related this account to Mother, she responded, "The poor boy has been tossed around most of his life, and he deserves better, but he's never given up. Thorsby Institute was good for him, and I think he will be okay."

JOYCE HOWARD WAS NAMED director of the Baptist Training Union (BTU) at church that year. He asked that they make me his associate. BTU was similar to Sunday School at night, and I had various duties to perform.

The Sunday after our band triumph in the spring, I helped lead the singing and reported on some statistics. Then we went to class, and Mr. Brausa went with me to the young adults. High school seniors were included in hopes the name of the class would influence their behavior.

I. H. McNeill, the class leader, had a bit of a mischievous streak. He had been figuring out a way to pull one on Mr. Brausa, and at the end of class he lowered the boom. "It's time for us to be dismissed," I. H. said. "Mr. Brausa, would you lead us in our closing prayer?"

Mr. Brausa froze in panic and choked. Finally, he managed to get out some words and put an "Amen" at the end. He headed out the door, and while he continued coming to the cafe on Sunday afternoons, he never again set foot in the Baptist Church.

FOR THE SPRING CONCERT that year, I played *Stars in a Velvety Sky*, one of Mr. Brausa's favorites. I heard him perform it between acts of a play, and it was so beautiful it brought tears to everybody's eyes. He loaned me his music. Since he didn't have a band arrangement, I had to be accompanied on the piano. He got Mary Clyde Mims, a senior at Chilton County High and one of my summer classmates, to play. Mary Clyde smiled, and in short order I was over my timidity. I forgot all about Louise Brown and started driving our new car to Clanton at every opportunity.

NOT LONG BEFORE THE school year ended, we heard that one of our teachers, Paralee Henson, was going to get married in a few weeks. Everyone in Jemison loved Paralee. Her father died when she was a baby, and her mother had to struggle mightily to make ends meet. By her own labor and will power, Paralee made it through college. Now she was going to marry a young lawyer.

The wedding was scheduled for the Baptist Church, and I was asked to be an usher. I was thrilled and not at all concerned when they announced it was to be formal.

On the wedding day I started putting on the tux Mother had rented. Everything went fine until I put on the shirt. The sleeves were about six inches too long and didn't have any buttons. I was in a panic until Bill Dubose came along and showed me how to fasten the French cuffs and put in the cufflinks.

THE SENIOR PLAY WAS one of the last events each year and was widely anticipated. Miss Harvey was the director. She chose *Professor How Could You?*, and at first I said I wasn't going to be in it. Miss Harvey needed an extra actor, and Mother finally persuaded me. I figured it was already the end of the year, and Mack was her pet, so I might as well do it. I played the role of the professor. Late in the third act, I came walking out wearing a dress and a wig. The audience erupted in wild laughter, and I just stood there, looking silly and not knowing what to do. The laughter lasted a good five minutes. This had been Robert Hall's idea, and he finally came and dragged me off the stage. Rescued!

AT LAST CAME THE night of graduation, which marked the climax of the school year. My time had finally arrived.

We all lined up in our caps and gowns. When the band started playing, we marched down the aisle. As we walked by them on the way to the stage, I gave the boy in my chair a little pat on the head.

The ceremony went along, with different awards given to different students. Finally, it was time for the grand award, "Most Outstanding Student," to be announced. The county superintendent of education opened the envelope and said, "It goes to our friend, John Hayman." There was a nice applause. Mother and Dad were very proud. The commencement speaker followed, and told us in a thousand ways we were stepping into the adult world.

We marched out, and the ceremony ended. I was standing in the hall with some of the other students, feeling good and pondering the fact that we were no longer in high school. Several people congratulated me for getting the award. The father of one of my classmates came walking over. I stuck out my hand to shake his, but he didn't take it. Instead, he looked at me with a frown and said, "I'll never know why they gave the big award to you."

I went home where Mother was having a little party. I was still a little stunned over the comment, but I didn't mention what had happened. Everybody was happy. Then Mrs. Reynolds stood up, took my right hand in hers, and said, "I want you to know, I've had you in any number of classes over seven years, and you have always been a pleasure to work with." Her eyes were misty, and she reached over and gave me a big kiss on the cheek. This restored my spirits. My classmate's father tried to lay a downer on me, and I reckoned that adults sometimes do such things. It hurt a little, but it didn't really do any long-term damage. All in all, it had been a very good day. I may not have known how to act or how to wear French cuffs, but one thing was sure, I had no choice but to continue to learn and move ahead. Childhood was gone forever.

Epilogue

I was home on leave after a year in Korea in the Air Force. I went to New Orleans and put into action a plan which had been years in the making. I bought a ticket to Cincinnati on the Hummingbird. It was a glorious ride. The train was beautiful and the services wonderful. It was everything I had dreamed.

After we flew through Clanton, I prepared myself. Ten miles later, with the Hummingbird going about a hundred miles an hour, I looked out the window to the east. There was the Jemison Cafe and not far behind it, a field on a hillside. In my mind's eye, I saw a wide-eyed boy watching the train, and in front of him a gray mule, happy for a brief respite. It was a great moment, the fulfillment of my childhood fantasy!

As JOEL WILLIAMSON POINTS out in *Crucible of Race*, the blacks were forced to develop a separate culture and their own set of social activities. Blacks and whites lived in close physical proximity in Jemison, but we lived separately. There were the "white" houses and the "quarters."

Blacks had their own churches, their own Masonic Lodge, their own Eastern Star, their own community leaders, their own everything. The only places they mixed with whites on an equal basis were where both stood, like the grocery store and the post office.

This was the way things were, and we didn't give it a second thought. One black family was very special to us, however, and that was Jack Sales, his wife Vicie, and their children, five of whom were Mother's helpers for twenty-five years. After the last one went her way, Vicie continued to work in the cafe.

One afternoon after the civil rights revolution was well under way, I was home from graduate school. I went by to sit with Jack on his front porch. We talked about this and that and finally came around to the racial violence then occurring. Jack said, "I don't understand it. All I want is to live peace-fully. I haven't done anything to make people want to hurt me. I guess if you're going to hold somebody down, you have to decide you hate them."

Mother was heartbroken a few years later when Vicie died. It was cus-tomary for whites to sit in the back when they attended a black church. At the funeral, the usher asked Mother if she would like to join the family in the front pew, and since she wanted to show her respect, she agreed. To her shock, about halfway through his sermon, the preacher asked Mother if she would say a few words. She told me later that she was so taken by surprise, she stammered, and was barely able to get a word out. She regained control of herself and told the congregation what Vicie and her family had meant to us. For a moment, skin color didn't matter.

JOE BRATTON BECAME A dentist and made a ton of money, just as he always planned. People tell me he is a great dentist, but remembering our project of dissecting a live frog would give me second thoughts of letting him work on me. He might remember our political differences.

Mack Smith majored in education and started his teaching career in Jemison. The best thing he did was marry a wonderful woman, Treva, who kept him on the straight and narrow.

Kenneth Ray stayed in the Navy more than twenty years. When he returned to Jemison to live, he had greatly honed his gift of gab and be-came a successful salesman. He built a house in one of the nicest sections of town. His rise to respectability in his home town was complete when he was elected mayor for several terms.

WAHOO CONTINUED TO PRACTICE his herb healing until he met his demise in December 1949. Two men robbed him. Wahoo, his son Bruce, and Earl Clecker gave chase to the robbers. When the robbers wrecked, a shoot-out occurred, and Wahoo was killed. James Lawley and William McDonald were captured, confessed, and were sentenced to prison.

UNCLE BUDDY AND AUNT Lena raised their eight children, all of whom continued their education and had successful careers and marriages. Aunt

Lena, Aunt Gladys, and Uncle Jimmy have departed this world.

BY SOME QUIRK OF fate, I always wound up living close to or working with Marvin Dawson Jr., the "Junior" of my youth. After college, he served in the Army, then used the G.I. Bill to earn a master's and a Ph.D. He had a fine career as an educator, and in 1972 was named Calloway Professor at Mercer University. He had a successful second career restoring and selling old, historic homes. Marvin raised three children, and currently resides in Georgia.

BARBARA AND JESSE TRAVELED to many far-away places, and spent ten years on Kwajalein Island in the South Pacific. Jesse obtained his doctorate and became a nationally recognized radar expert. They raised four children, and have retired to Huntsville, Alabama.

I HAD THE WANDERLUST after I left the Air Force, and lived in seven different states, from New York to California. I also had the good fortune to live and work in Paris, France. I always enjoyed learning about other parts of the world, but as I advanced in years, I felt the "salmon instinct" to return to Alabama. I wound up in Birmingham, just a stone's throw from Jemison.

I have three children, Becky, Edie, and Johnny, and two granddaughters, Rachael and Kira.

DAD'S HEALTH CONTINUED TO decline, and he died of a stroke in 1964. My mother died, after a short bout with Alzheimer's disease, on February 17, 1987, shortly after her eighty-second birthday. I'll never be able to put into words what their love and support meant to me. I guess most people who grow up in a close family feel the same way about their parents. We never say enough when they are with us, but maybe, wherever they are, they know how we feel.

JEMISON IS LIKE THOUSANDS of other small towns in the United States, but then, it's not. To me, it's unique. It's my home town. The memories of my youth there and the people I grew up with are dear to my heart. They were wonderful people, not given to debating the subtle nuances of political and theological theory, but warm and caring. Most important to me, my home town was the location of that marvelous institution which saved our family in a time of crisis and became the center of our existence, the Jemison Cafe.

~

Postscript

The majority of the folks in this true story have since died: Uncle Buddy; Mr. and Mrs. Reynolds; Mr. and Mrs. Howard; Jack Sales; Mr. and Mrs. Dubose; Billy Ellison; Reid Adams; Kenneth Ray; Coach Turner; and others. Marvin (Junior) Dawson Jr. is also gone. There is no doubt John loved them all.

After John's stint in the Air Force during the Korean War, he used the G.I. Bill to obtain a master's degree from Syracuse University and a Ph.D. from Stanford University. He had successful careers in college teaching, research, and writing. John was also fortunate enough to travel around the world for business and pleasure and to work in Paris, France. He thought that was "pretty good for a Jemison boy."

He continued to play the cornet until the end of his life.

— CLARA RUTH HAYMAN HOLT

www.ingramcontent.com/pod-product-compliance
Lightning Source LLC
Chambersburg PA
CBHW022024090426
42739CB00006BA/270